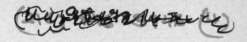

The
Awakened One

The
Awakened One

The Life and Work of
Bhagwan Shree Rajneesh

VASANT JOSHI
(Swami Satya Vedant)

1817

Harper & Row, Publishers, San Francisco

Cambridge, Hagerstown, New York, Philadelphia
London, Mexico City, São Paulo, Sydney

FIRST EDITION

Designer: Jim Mennick

Library of Congress Cataloging in Publication Data

Joshi, Vasant, 1941–
    THE AWAKENED ONE.

    Bibliography: p. 204
    1. Rajneesh, Acharya, 1931–   2. Gurus—United States—Biography.
I. Title.
BP605.S553R344   1982   299'.93 [B]   81- 48209
ISBN 0-06-064205-X   AACR2

82 83 84 85 86 10 9 8 7 6 5 4 3 2 1

*To Dadda and Mataji
and to my children,
Nipun and Anuja*

Contents

Preface

I HAD my first *darshan* (audience) with Bhagwan Shree Rajneesh at Shree Rajneesh Ashram, Poona, India, on January 11, 1975. Ever since that time I have experienced his continuous flow of love and compassion for me. In the same darshan Bhagwan initiated me into *sannyas* (discipleship) and then asked me to write a book on him. The offer came as a complete surprise to me. I nodded, however, in affirmation, with awe and deep gratitude. I returned to Chicago after attending the ten-day meditation camp.

In 1979, Bhagwan asked me to come and stay in the Rajneesh Ashram with my family—an opportunity I had longed for since the initiation. During the two-year stay I immensely enjoyed working on the biography as well as carrying out my other assignments at the ashram.

I am very grateful to the Rajneesh Foundation International for extending to me all the necessary assistance in completing this project while leaving me free to tell this story of the first fifty years of Bhagwan's life in my own way. Neither Bhagwan nor anyone else from the Shree Rajneesh Ashram has approved or even looked at the text —it is strictly a personal and independent account of Bhagwan's life and work.

I am indeed thankful to my friend F. Lanier Graham for his encouragement and support. I am also greatly indebted to Gary Matkin for giving me his valuable time and making helpful and constructive comments on the manuscript and for helping me in every possible way in the completion of this book.

I would like to acknowledge special thanks to Clayton Carlson, Marie Cantlon, John Loudon, and Tom Dorsaneo.

My sincere thanks to all those *sannyasins* (my fellow disciples) who helped me in this project.

Introduction

THIS IS the official biography of Bhagwan Shree Rajneesh written by one of his devoted disciples. Bhagwan is an enlightened master who lived his life in India until coming to America in 1981. He has attracted many thousands of disciples from all parts of the world. Although I have called it a biography, much of the material for this story consists of Bhagwan's own words faithfully tape-recorded by his disciples—a total of four thousand hours of discourse, transcribed and edited from lectures delivered every morning by Bhagwan from 1974 to 1981. Although Bhagwan has used autobiographical vignettes in these discourses to illustrate and communicate his spiritual message, he finds no use in writing an autobiography. Once, when asked, "Why do you not write your autobiography?" Bhagwan answered: ". . . truly speaking, after self-knowledge there is no autobiography. All autobiographies are 'ego-biographies.' What we call an autobiography is not the story of the soul. As long as you do not know what soul is, whatever you write is ego-biography."[1]

This is an attempt to communicate the truth of Bhagwan's life and the truth of his experience. But while the external facts of his life do contribute to communicating this truth, they can only convey a shadowlike picture of an enlightened person. As Bhagwan himself has explained, one who has known himself as a soul and not as a person

. . . changes into something so formless that what we call the facts of his life, facts like the date he was born, the date a particular event happened, dissolve. What happens is that all these facts cease to have any meaning. The awakening of a soul is so cataclysmic that after it occurs, when one opens his eyes he finds that everything is lost. . . .

After one has known one's soul, an autobiography seems to be a dreamlike version of oneself. It is as if one were writing an account of his dreams: one day he saw this dream, the next day that dream, and the day after that a third dream. Such an autobiography has no more value than a fantasy, a fairy tale.[2]

Despite this view expressed directly from my Master, I have found it valuable to know about Bhagwan's life, for his life is his teaching. Once in centuries comes such a being who by his own living creates an energy that brings individuals to a point where they begin to see a new vision, feel the richness and beauty of existence, and enjoy the mysteries of life. Bhagwan, through his love, inspires thousands to break away from their conditioned past and live in the moment—in freedom and awareness. Bhagwan is the "awakened one," the "enlightened one,"—the one who has seen "that which is" through pure consciousness and not through any mental projection, one who has become aware that the source of divine power is within oneself, that misery is the creation of the mind, and that the mind can be transcended. Even though the experience of his awakening is beyond verbal description, what little we may know of it can awaken us to the causes of our own miseries and help us find the source of joy and divinity that lies within us. As Bhagwan says:

. . . The matter of the experience of becoming aware remains, but what is known through the experience cannot be written down. This is so because reducing such an experience to words makes it seem insipid and absurd. Even so, there is always the attempt to tell about the experience in different ways through different methods. . . . My purpose is to take you on that path that may lead you to the experience itself. . . . The best way is to carry you on that path, to that bank, from which you can be pushed to where someday you yourself may have the experience.[3]

My purpose, however, is not to evaluate Bhagwan's teachings critically in any historical context, or against a background of any particular school of thought, philosophy, tradition, or movement. My aim is to present the story of Bhagwan's life as it became available to me from various sources.

It is my hope that this biography will serve as an introduction to Bhagwan for those who are interested in him and in the spiritual path. But it can be no more than that. One must experience Bhagwan through his books, taped lectures, video tapes, or best of all—in person. Only then will this story really mean something to the reader.

1. Who Is
Bhagwan Shree Rajneesh?

To HIS thousands of disciples all over the world he is known simply as "Bhagwan"—the "Blessed One." He is their Master, the "living flame" of a new religious consciousness. To the people in India he has been known as "Acharya Rajneesh," the fiery teacher who destroys age-old myths and beliefs, traditions and teachings. "I teach utter rebellion," he declares. "I am not here to compromise. I have decided to be utterly honest and truthful whatsoever the cost. If we want to change society, society is going to be offended."[1]

He tears apart the conventional concepts of nationalism and racial superiority, refutes Marx and socialistic ideas, criticizes Freud and Jung, cracks jokes at the pope in the Vatican and at Shankaracharya of Puri, the religious head of the Hindus, and does not disguise his contempt for politicians. The Hindus condemn him as a hedonist, the Communists belittle him as a spiritualist, the journalists describe him as a "sex guru," and one scholar called him "the Hugh Heffner of the spiritual world." Bhagwan brushes aside all these labels. "I am a materialist-spiritualist," he says. "I teach a sensuous religion. I want Gautam the Buddha and Zorba the Greek to come closer and closer; my disciple has to be Zorba-the-Buddha. Man is body-soul together. Both have to be satisfied."

In his spontaneous daily morning discourses he has

spoken on a variety of subjects: from birth to death and beyond, from politics to prayer, from nuclear physics to Jungian philosophy, from holistic health to new education, from sex to superconsciousness. In over two thousand discourses since 1974, Bhagwan has covered a full spectrum of human inquiry through his insight into the various spiritual paths possible for humans. He has put the messages of the various spiritual traditions in a modern context. He has spoken on Zen, Sufi, Taoist, and Hassidic masters; on the sayings of Buddha, Mahavir, Jesus, Lao Tzu, Chuang Tzu, Heraclitus, Pythagoras, Kabir, and Nanak, as well as on such Indian scriptures as the *Bhagavad Gita,* the *Upanishads,* the *Yoga Sutras* of Patanjali, the *Dhammapada,* and the songs of tantric mystics.

His outspoken and critical discourses have aroused a great deal of anger and opposition against him around the world. His ideas on such sensitive issues as sex, marriage, family, and relationships attack the conventional view of these things. But the greatest target of public disapproval is the full freedom he allows his disciples. He encourages his disciples to go deeply and totally into all the experiences of life. He extends this freedom to sex as well as mental states such as violence, jealousy, possessiveness, greed, hatred, and others that make up the whole range of human emotions.

Such freedom, particularly with regard to sex, has been the main cause for the opposition to Bhagwan in India. For generations Indian priests and holy men have preached that the divine is attainable only through the denial of sex, while Bhagwan holds exactly the opposite viewpoint. He asserts that only by experiencing sex fully can we enjoy it, understand it, and most importantly for our spiritual growth, even transcend it. Transcendence can never be achieved through denial or suppression, he says. He points out repeatedly that the door to liberation, or *moksha,* lies beyond the experience and understanding of our passions.

Bhagwan cites Mahatma Gandhi as an example of how misdirected the path of celibacy and asceticism can be. "Gandhi renounced sex and repressed it his whole life," he explains. "Only in his last years did he become aware of the repression, because his sexual fantasies continued. Then he started experimenting with Tantra, but it was too late."

In misunderstanding the teachings of Bhagwan people have ignored Bhagwan's repeated warnings to his disciples about the danger of becoming indulgent. He places one stringent restriction upon the exercising of complete freedom: "I give you total freedom to experience, with just one condition: be alert, be watchful, be conscious."

The movement around Bhagwan has attracted thousands of people from all over the world who come to him to explore their previously repressed emotions and experience catharsis under the guidance of professionally trained Western therapists. The uniqueness of these therapy groups and the controversy surrounding them has drawn people to Bhagwan from many different parts of the world: North and South America, Europe, Australia, New Zealand, and Japan. This international movement includes people from many professions and walks of life: lawyers, physicians, psychologists, educators, scientists, dentists, acupuncturists, businessmen, administrators, journalists, writers, artists, architects, photographers, radical feminists, New Age seekers, "flower children," housewives, and Catholic priests are represented. About forty percent of the disciples are of Jewish descent. Most of Bhagwan's disciples are young—between the ages of twenty and forty. "I want to rely on youth . . . " declares Bhagwan:

They are coming by breaking all the barriers. Future is not created by old people, future is created by youth. Whenever any religion is alive then it attracts youth. Whenever any religion dies it attracts old people. Where religion is still alive, and where new rays are showering, and where a new flower is opening its petals, there you will find youth. Now any person who has become old in spirit cannot remain here; only youth can be here.

After being initiated into *sannyas* at a *darshan*,[2] the disciple of Bhagwan is called a *sannyasin*. In the Hindu tradition a sannyasin is one who has renounced the family and material world, according to Hindu rites, and has become a monk. Bhagwan views this tradition as negative and escapist and substitutes his own meaning for a sannyasin—one who accepts and affirms life, who participates actively and joyfully in life. In Bhagwan's vision, a sannyasin is one who does not renounce the family, the society, or possessions; instead, he gives up his ego-attachment to them, he drops his passion for and possessiveness of them. The movement is known therefore as the "neo-sannyas" movement. (A detailed description of this movement will be given later.)

A disciple of Bhagwan is identified by four things: orange-colored clothing symbolizing the rising sun, freshness, and growth; the *mala,* or necklace,[3] from which hangs a locket containing Bhagwan's picture, which serves as a reminder to the wearer of his or her commitment to Bhagwan; a new name, which represents a break with the past; and a daily meditation appropriate for the individual disciple.

The new name given to a disciple by Bhagwan is preceded by the title "Swami" for men and "Ma" for women. "Ma" means "mother" and emphasizes receptivity, openness, and intuition. It indicates, according to Bhagwan, "the ultimate flowering of a woman." The word "Swami" means "lord." "I have called you Swami just to indicate your path—so you become lord of yourself. It is not to make others slaves to you, it is just to make a master of you," explains Bhagwan.

Reared on a philosophy of struggle and competition, success and power, but disillusioned with this self-destructive approach to life, Westerners in particular listen to Bhagwan's message with great relief and gratitude. Their whole gestalt changes—from aggression to receptivity, from struggle to surrender and joyful acceptance. For many years now Western psychology has been moving away from the analytical to the holistic approach, unifying the body and the emotions. This new psychology has its roots in the "human potential movement," or "growth movement." Americans and Europeans find that becoming a sannyasin adds a spiritual dimension to the physical and emotional aspects of their searching.

To surrender to a Spiritual Master such as Bhagwan is not to surrender to his personal power; it is a surrender to the divine energy of which he has become a vehicle. Bhagwan should not be seen as a superman and he does not claim to be one. He is not interested in creating a race of superhumans. In a spiritual context, the man who calls himself "Bhagwan," meaning "God" in English, is not a person who has assumed a mantle of God, but rather a human being who has perceived the unity and wholeness of existence and has transcended all dualities. Such a person has become whole, or holy. Once, when asked, "Do you consider yourself God?" Bhagwan replied with humor, "No, sir, certainly not! Even if I were I would have denied it, because who will take responsibility for this ugly world? I cannot take responsibility for creating you! That will be the real original sin!"

To the Western mind it is difficult to conceive that a person presently living is a god or has powers normally associated with God, since God has been seen as the creator, a father figure. In this role "God," while he may be seen as personal and directly approachable by humans, is experienced essentially as the "other," as separate and having a separate existence. Bhagwan does not see the phenomenon in such dualistic terms. He explains that God does not exist separately as a creator of this world, because the creation, the creator, and the creativity are one. Existence is one, he says, the whole existence is divine. Just as the dance and the dancer are inseparable, so too are the creation and the creator.

To a similar question, "Why do you call yourself Bhagwan?" ("Why do you call yourself God?"), he replied, "Because I am. And because you are. And because only God is.... The whole consists of one stuff.... If you can recognize God in me, you have taken the first step toward recognizing him in yourself."

Explaining the meaning of the Sanskrit term "Bhagwan," he says:

The Indian term for God ("Bhagwan") simply means "the blessed one": one who is fortunate enough to recognize his own being. It has nothing to do with creating the world—I deny all responsibility!—it simply means one who has recognized himself as divine.

Bhagwan moved to the six-acre *ashram*[4] located in a residential area of Poona, India (a city eighty miles southeast of Bombay) in 1974. Before that he lived in an apartment in Bombay from 1970 to 1974. He was well known even then throughout India for his fiery, controversial talks, but was unheard of outside India. Some British and American psychotherapists who had come to India in search of new insights into personal growth were among the first Westerners to come in contact with Bhagwan in Bombay. They found him an enlightened mystic, an authentic human being, a loving Master who was ready to help people transcend their unconscious, conditioned behavior patterns and flow toward the state of Buddhahood or enlightenment.

Enlightenment is a word freely used these days in spiritual, growth-oriented circles. Bhagwan promises his sannyasins neither enlightenment nor bliss. He says these have to be earned by each individual by working through one's conditioning and confronting pain—bliss and enlightenment cannot be given or transferred. To assist disciples on the path, Bhagwan has designed and introduced many new techniques of meditation, of which Dynamic Meditation is the primary technique. (See Appendix A for an annotated list of some of these meditations.) Because people today live a chronically cerebral and repressed life, Bhagwan emphasizes total, dynamic methods of meditation involving the entire body/mind unity. They are aimed at shattering social and psychological conditioning and at relieving countless suppressed emotions and impulses by vigorous, cathartic methods, so that one may experience the silent, meditative state.

Most of the management and control of this growing movement is in the hands of women. Bhagwan has deliberately put women in the positions of authority. "I don't want the ashram run by the intellect," he explains:

I want it run by the female heart, because to me, to be feminine is to become vulnerable, to become receptive. To be feminine is to become passive; to be feminine is to allow; to be feminine is to wait. To be feminine is not to be tense and in a hurry; to be feminine is to be in love. Yes, the ashram is run by women because I want it to be run by the heart.

Journalists from the West have often tried to find parallels between what happened in Jonestown and the movement growing around Bhagwan. "Could such a thing happen again?" they ask.

Bhagwan sees all orthodox religions as anti-life, as death-oriented. In his view, the horror of Jonestown was an outcome of the life-negative attitude perpetuated by established religions. Bhagwan's response to the Jonestown phenomenon is as follows:

I would like to say this to the whole world: you have no right to condemn Jones, because that is what all your churches and all your temples have been teaching down through the ages. Rever-

end Jones died in the American way—fast and quick—that's all.
Only I can condemn him . . . because I teach life.

Bhagwan says he teaches his disciples a totally different
kind of death—the death of the ego as taught by Buddha
and Jesus and all other enlightened beings of the East and
the West. "I am for the death of the mind, not of the
body," he says. "I am saying, die every moment; die to the
past; understand that every moment is a new birth. In that
freshness you will relate to God."

The following chapters present the life story of a man
who has experienced the death of the ego, the transcendence of mind, and the realization of that which is real. His
compassion for his fellow human beings is as strong and
pervasive as is his passion for truth. He goes to extraordinary lengths to share the experience and joy of his own
awakening with anyone who is ready to listen, anyone who
is tired of sleep and disillusioned with dreams.

2. Birth and Family

BHAGWAN'S father, Babulal (known affectionately later as Dadda), was born in Timarni in 1908 into a Digambara Jain family.[1] Timarni was and still is a small town of about six thousand people in Madhya Pradesh, a state situated in the heart of India, in the Vindhyachal mountain range. The gracious river Narmada runs through the state.

Bhagwan's grandfather came from a large family that lived originally in a small town called Basoda. Basoda was once hit by a plague and the entire population was exposed to the epidemic. A few members of the family died in it. Many, including Dadda's father and uncle, escaped with their families. They fled to Timarni where the in-laws of Dadda's uncle lived. Dadda's aunt also lived in Timarni. She helped Dadda's father by loaning him a few rupees to buy cloth. With this help he started a small business of his own. He would load his horse with cloth and sell it in the villages. Later, this aunt arranged Dadda's father's marriage and found him a house to rent.

As the family grew, their financial situation became more and more critical. Dadda's father decided to leave Timarni and try his luck somewhere else. One day he loaded his cart with all his belongings and set out with the family to Kuchwada where the parents of his wife lived. Between Timarni and Kuchwada lay the town of Gadarwara. The family stopped here. Though the town was not very big, it was quite prosperous—it was the biggest grain-producing center in the area. Dadda's father decided to try his business in this town, so in 1934 they settled down in Gadarwara. (Rajneesh was already three years old by then, but we shall pick up the story of his birth a little later in the chapter.)

Dadda and his father worked hard to make their cloth business a success. Bhagwan's grandfather enjoyed his business and maintained the human touch in his dealings. Bhagwan has a very fond memory of it:

I remember my old grandfather. He was a cloth merchant and I and my whole family were puzzled because he enjoyed it so much. For hours together it was a game with the customers. If something was worth ten rupees, he would ask fifty rupees for it, and he knew this was absurd. And his customers knew it too; they knew that it must be near about ten rupees, and they would start from two rupees. Then a long haggling would follow—hours together. My father and my uncles would get angry. . . . But he [grandfather] had his own customers. When they came, they would ask, "Where is Dada,"[2] where is grandfather? Because with him [grandfather] it is a game, a play, whether we lost one rupee or two, whether it is more or less, that is not the point! They [customers] enjoyed it.[3]

Dadda wanted to pursue his formal education but had to give up the idea after the fourth grade in order to help his father in the business. However, he strongly encouraged his two younger brothers to continue their schooling uninterrupted—even against the wishes of his father who wanted them to help in the business also. Dadda secretly provided money to his younger brother Amritlal[4] so that Amritlal could finish high school and move to the city of Jabalpur[5] for his college education. This caused Dadda some family trouble. In 1932 Amritlal took part in India's independence movement led by Gandhi and was imprisoned. When Dadda's father and other family members heard about it, they were shocked—the very idea of someone in the family going to prison caused tremendous uproar and unhappiness. Bhagwan's grandfather was very angry at Dadda because he blamed Dadda for it—if Dadda had not helped Amritlal, Amritlal would not have gotten in trouble and been imprisoned.

Dadda's two brothers, Amritlal and Shikharchand, were important early influences on Rajneesh. Amritlal's literary talent and activities made him an early model for Rajneesh, who began to express himself by composing poems. However, Rajneesh was closer to the younger uncle, Shikharchand. Shikharchand became an active member of the Congress Party and was inspired by its progressive thinking. He believed in the ideas of socialism and was responsible for seeking application of them in the town of Gadarwara—the ideas had an effect on young Rajneesh for quite a time. With Shikharchand he organized several group meetings of young men and inspired them to accept socialistic ideas. Because of his active participation in political movements, Shikharchand could not continue his studies beyond high school.

Dadda remained determined throughout his life to encourage others to pursue education. In fact, in his own family, he helped his children earn degrees in medicine, engineering, and science.

A description of Dadda, particularly of his personal qualities, is important to this story, not only because it sheds some light on Bhagwan's early years, but also because Bhagwan often uses his father's qualities as examples in his teachings. Bhagwan's father was indeed a lovable man. He was well known in the town of Gadarwara in his several roles as head of his family, businessman, and a citizen of Gadarwara. His simplicity, kindness, wisdom, and sense of humor came through so clearly that no one who met him could fail to be affected and impressed by him.

Two personal qualities stood out in Dadda. First, he was very fond of nature. His routine included morning walks along the river and at least a couple of hours of swimming in it. Bhagwan's earliest memories of his father are associated with those daily walks with him.

The first thing I remember about him is that he would wake me up at three o'clock in the morning. I was very young then, when three o'clock was a sleeping time. . . . He would wake me at three o'clock and take me for a walk. That was his first gift to me—the *Brahma Muhurta*.[6] In the beginning it bothered me a lot. I used to practically drag behind him . . . but gradually I began to see and feel the beauty of early morning hours. Gradually I came to realize that the moments of the early morning are not meant to be lost. Perhaps God is never so close to the earth at any other time as he is during these early morning moments.[7]

Second, Dadda was very friendly and generous to everyone. Another early memory that Bhagwan has of his father is related to his father's lavish spending on friends and guests, even though he himself was not a wealthy man. Every day he had guests for dinner, even if it meant that he had to borrow money. His object in life seemed to be sharing. Bhagwan recalls one incident:

Once he incurred a great deal of loss. I asked him if he would be able to bear such a loss. He said, "I can never go in loss, because my father left me with only seven hundred rupees. As long as they are safe, I need not worry—the rest can come and go. These seven hundred," he said, "will never be lost"—he was sure about it. I asked him to control his spending, but to no avail—the parties and dinners continued. The process of sharing went on uninterrupted.[8]

Dadda also took active interest in helping needy people, financially and in other ways. He had a progressive mind and was prepared to depart from social mores even at the risk of ostracism. But above all, Dadda was a spiritual man. According to his younger brother Amritlal, Dadda had a reputation as a religious person. He used to visit the temple, fast and read scriptures. But this was just the outer side—inwardly, his search continued for that which cannot be confined to a temple, book, or a ritual. For the last ten years of life he meditated regularly from three to six o'clock in the morning. Dadda lived his last years at the Shree Rajneesh Ashram in Poona, often going so deeply into meditation for five or six hours that Bhagwan's mother would get worried and try to wake him up in time for Bhagwan's morning discourse at eight o'clock. On several occasions Dadda remained in meditation and missed the discourse.

Bhagwan's mother, Saraswatibai, is sixty-seven years old. People ask her questions about Bhagwan and his life when he was young, and she answers them openly and unassumingly. She expresses her feelings about the questions she is continually asked:

I wonder why he [Bhagwan] took birth in this simple family [of ours], because people go on asking so many meaningful questions, and Bhagwan talks with such wisdom . . . and [here] we are full of amazement at why should he have taken birth in this family! If we had been more talented parents we could have described so many things about [his life] . . . would have complimented him in so many ways. But we cannot. We feel stunned when these questions come. People pour questions, but we do not feel capable of answering them.[9]

She has always been a kind hostess. She is known for her loving hospitality, for having been a perfect match to her husband who tremendously enjoyed entertaining friends, relatives, and others.

Saraswati was an only child and hence very dear to her parents. Kuchwada, where they lived, is a small farming village with a population of about seven hundred. It is located in the beautiful valley of the Vindhya Mountains in Madhya Pradesh. Her father was comparatively wealthy and a very kind person. In addition to farming, he operated a small grocery store. In the past, child marriages were common in India and Bhagwan's mother was married when she was a mere child. This practice sometimes had a humorous side, as Bhagwan recounts:

When my mother got married, she was only seven years old. I was asking her again and again, "Tell me how you felt?" She said, "I didn't know what was happening. I was simply joyous that something was happening. I used to run out to see what was happening, and they would pull me back inside the house. And they locked me in on the day when the real ceremony was going to happen,[10] because I was so much interested in the bands and the music and the horses. And the people were coming . . . " And I asked my father, 'What did you feel?" He said, "I don't know—I just enjoyed the horse ride."[11]

It was from the union of these two loving, simple, and open people that on December 11, 1931, at her parents' home in Kuchwada, Saraswati gave birth to a very beautiful, healthy child. The mother was enormously happy at the birth of her first baby—a boy. The new mother's parents were also overjoyed, especially the new grandfather. The grace and beauty of the child convinced the grandfather that a king of some past life had taken birth in their family, so he spontaneously named him "Raja," meaning "the king."[12] Saraswati's father loved his grandson so much that he would not allow her to take him back to Timarni, where she lived with Dadda and his father's family in their struggling cloth business. As Bhagwan describes it:

My early childhood passed at the house of my maternal grandparents and I had great love for them. . . . They were feeling very lonely, so they wanted to bring me up. Therefore, I stayed with them up to seven years of age. I had taken them as my mother and father. They were very rich and had all possible conveniences. Therefore, I was brought up like a prince. I came in touch with my father and mother only after the death of my maternal grandparents. . . . I had loved only them, and received love only from them.[13]

Raja (Rajneesh) was occasionally brought to Timarni. Bhagwan's youngest uncle, Shikharchand, still remembers that wonderful experience when Raja was brought to Timarni for the first time when he was about six months old. Shikharchand was the first one to receive and hold the child. He greeted the beautiful baby with immense joy. Later it was he who gave Raja a new name: Rajneesh Chandra Mohan. Until his enrollment in school, the boy was called Raja; after that people began to call him Rajneesh.

The birth of Rajneesh was not of an ordinary kind, for it was the birth of one who had walked on this earth before in search of Truth. He had traveled numerous paths before, through many schools and systems. His last birth was seven hundred years ago in the mountains where he had a mystic school that attracted disciples of many traditions and paths from faraway lands. The Master lived to be one hundred six years old. Prior to his death he entered into a twenty-one-day fast that would have brought him enlightenment when finished. But he had the option of taking one more birth before finally disappearing in the eternal. He looked at his family of disciples; there were many who were still on their way, needing help. He also saw the great potential for bringing about a synthesis between East and West, body and soul, materialism and spiritualism. He saw the possibility of creating a new man—a man of the future totally discontinuous with the past. He, who had come so close to the ultimate achievement for which he had worked so hard for so many lives, decided to come back again into a human body. Out of pure love and compassion he promised his disciples that he would return and share his truth with them and bring their consciousness to a state of awakening.

The fascinating account of Bhagwan's previous birth came to light accidentally; Bhagwan himself had not mentioned it to anyone. However, years ago when his mother was visiting Mr. Ramlal Pungalia (presently a disciple of Bhagwan) in Poona, he, out of curiosity, asked her if she remembered anything peculiar about her son's childhood. She told him that after birth Rajneesh did not cry or take any milk for three days.

I raised the same question once again to Bhagwan's mother during my interviews with her in October, 1979, and asked if she recalled anything more than what she had related earlier to Mr. Pungalia. She described the incident as follows:

Yes, he did not take milk for three days. I was very much worried, but did not know what to do. My mother was looking after him. She kept feeding him water and told me not to worry. On the fourth day, after my mother gave him a good bath, he started taking milk.

I asked her if during those three days the child showed signs of any discomfort, to which she replied, "Not at all, his health remained normal all through these three days."[14]

Bhagwan explains this unusual circumstance:

This is true. Seven hundred years ago, in my previous life, there was a spiritual practice of twenty-one days, to be done before death. I was to give up my body after a total fast of twenty-one days. There were reasons for this, but I could not complete those twenty-one days. Three days remained. Those three days I had to complete in this life. This life is a continuity from there . . .

When only three days remained in that life, I was killed. Twenty-one days could not be completed because I was killed just three days before, and those three days were omitted. In this life, those three days were completed [by taking milk only on the fourth day].[15]

The killing, according to Bhagwan, did not result out of any enmity or hostility. "I have told many times in various discussions," says Bhagwan, "that just as Judas tried for a long time to kill Jesus, though Judas had no enmity with

Jesus, the person who killed me had no enmity with me, though he was taken to be and was treated as an enemy." Bhagwan continues:

That killing became valuable. At the time of death, those three days were left. After all my strenuous efforts for enlightenment during that life, I was able to achieve in this life, after a period of twenty-one years, that which had been possible to achieve during those three days. For each of those three days in that life, I had to spend seven years in this life.[16]

The fascinating account of Bhagwan's previous life seven hundred years ago opens up the whole issue of whether or not there is rebirth after death, or whether or not there is any basis for the theory of reincarnation. Bhagwan's explanation of it is based on his personal experience which is of significance to those seriously seeking the spiritual path and also to those who are working in the areas of parapsychology and altered states of consciousness.

How is a person reborn again into a new body? How is a Buddha reborn? How was Bhagwan reborn after a gap of seven hundred years? How did he measure the space of time between his last birth and this one? These are some of the questions to which Bhagwan has given elaborate answers. "I have an insider's view," says Bhagwan. "A Buddha has an insider's view. When a man like Buddha is born, he is born perfectly aware. When a man like Buddha is in the womb, he is aware."[17]

Normally death occurs in a state of unconsciousness, a state in which the dying person is totally incapable of experiencing or witnessing the occurrence of death. Witnessing it is possible only if one has experienced deep meditation, where one can see his or her body separate from consciousness. Bhagwan explains how it is to die and be reborn in full awareness:

If you can die in this life fully aware, not becoming unconscious when you die—you remain perfectly conscious, you see every phase of death, you hear every step and remain perfectly aware that the body is dying, the mind is disappearing and you remain perfectly aware—then suddenly you see that you are not in the body and consciousness has left the body. You can see the dead body lying there and you are floating around the body.

If you can be aware while you are dying, this is one part of birth, one aspect. If in this one aspect you are aware, you will be aware when you take conception. You will float around a couple making love and you will be perfectly aware. You will enter into the womb perfectly aware. The child is conceived aware of what is happening. For nine months in the mother's womb you will be aware. Not only will you be aware, but when a child like Buddha is in the womb of the mother, the quality of the mother changes. She becomes more aware . . . the mother immediately feels a change of consciousness.[18]

Speaking from his own experience, Bhagwan agrees with both Buddha and Mahavir that the two greatest forms of suffering are birth and death. But in Bhagwan's view the pain of birth is much more intense and fundamental than that of death. Speaking about the pain of birth he says:

If you can trust me, I say that the pain is greater than death. . . . And it should be so because birth makes death possible. . . . Birth is the beginning of suffering, death is the end. Birth has to be more painful—it is! And after nine months of total rest, relaxation, no worry, nothing to do, after those nine months it is such a sudden shock to be thrown out, that never again will there be such a shock to the nervous system, never again![19]

Bhagwan had to face difficulties in being born once again. The biggest obstacle was locating a suitable womb. "For any person who reaches a certain stage of development," he says, "it is difficult to find suitable parents for another birth."[20] Because people generally exhibited higher spiritual qualities during the times of Mahavir and Buddha, they did not have to face such difficulty, explains Bhagwan; advanced souls could easily find suitable wombs. In the case of Bhagwan, the prevalent decline in spiritual consciousness made it necessary for him to wait for the appropriate time, until in Dadda and Saraswati he was able to find ideal parents because of their spiritual qualities, loving nature, and higher consciousness.

Bhagwan explains further how he calculated the gap of seven hundred years. He distinguishes first, however, between the nature of time measurement when an advanced soul is in the body and when it is only a consciousness:

Time measurement begins only with the body. Outside the body, it makes no difference whether you have been for seven hundred years or seven thousand years. Only upon acquiring the body does the difference begin.[21]

Hence, in order to figure out the gap between his last death and present birth, he had to use an indirect method: he calculated the time by observing those who were with him in his past life and who may have been reborn several times since then.

Suppose, for example, that a particular person was known to me during my lifetime seven hundred years ago. In between there was a gap about me, but he may have taken birth ten times. However, there are memories of his past ten births. From his memories only can I calculate how long I must have remained without a body.[22]

Distinguishing between the time measured when one is in the body and when one is in the bodiless state, Bhagwan says:

It is near about like this, that for a moment I go to sleep and see a dream. In the dream I see that years have passed, and after some moments you awaken me and say that I have been dozing. . . . In a dream, an expanse of several years can be seen within a moment. The time scale of dream life is different. If, after awakening from a dream, the dreamer had no way of knowing when he slept, then it would be difficult to determine the length of time of his sleep. That can be known only by a clock: for example, when I was previously awake it was twelve o'clock, and now that I have gotten up after sleeping it is only one minute past twelve. Otherwise, I can only know because you were here also; there is no other way of knowing. So only in this way has it been determined that seven hundred years have passed.[23]

Bhagwan emphasizes that, in terms of spiritual growth, it is essential for individuals to know about their past lives so that they can begin their search from where they left off before. It can save a significant amount of energy and time in pursuing the search in the present life.

Therefore, what little I have told you about my previous life is not because it has any value or that you may know something about me. I have told you this only because it may make you reflect about yourself and set you in search of your past lives. The moment you know your past lives, there will be a spiritual revolution and evolution. Then you will start from where you had left off in your last life; otherwise, you will get lost in endless lives and reach nowhere. There will only be a repetition.[24]

As we continue our story in the next chapter we find that Rajneesh grew up just as any normal child would, and yet there was something very different, very unique that distinguished him from other children. One of the characteristics that attracts our attention is his tendency—right from an early age—to experiment. His interest in people, his keen observation of human nature, his creativity, and his own search for the Real were factors that contributed to his experiencing life directly and authentically. His search gave him extraordinary insights into the world around him and into the human psyche. With each insight he came closer and closer to the ultimate realization of That Which Is.

3. Youth:
The Years of Adventure

EVEN AS a child, Rajneesh exhibited a thirst for truth. His search was significantly influenced by the numerous encounters he had with death. He first experienced the shock of death at the age of five when his younger sister Kusum died; Rajneesh was very fond of her. He was so upset at her death that he refused food and insisted on behaving as a traditional Jain monk, wearing a loin cloth and carrying a begging bowl. His mother describes the scene:

He would ask us to sit in a row with food. Then, wearing monk-like clothes, he would walk from one end to another begging food with a bowl in his hand.[1]

It was only after considerable persuasion that little Rajneesh was able to resume his normal activities.

Most of the numerous close encounters Rajneesh has had with his own death were part of his own experiments. Three of the most significant of these were predicted by an astrologer. Rajneesh's grandfather had consulted a very famous astrologer who, after looking at the astrological chart of Rajneesh, predicted that the child would not survive beyond the seventh year. He did not consider it worthwhile, therefore, to continue drawing a chart for a person destined for such a short life. The astrologer himself died later on, but his son continued to work on Rajneesh's birth chart. The son too was puzzled and declared finally that the child would face death every seven years and that he would almost certainly die at the age of twenty-one. These predictions naturally worried Rajneesh's parents and family.

And, as Bhagwan points out, the astrologers were right, in a way. Seven, fourteen, and twenty-one were the years in which Bhagwan had deeper and deeper experiences with death. We shall deal here only with the events and experiences of Rajneesh's seventh and fourteenth years. The experience at the age of twenty-one, the ultimate experience, the culmination of the previous death experiences, will be described in Chapter 4.

Speaking of this first, most profound experience of death, Bhagwan says:

At the age of seven I survived, but I had a deep experience of death—not of my own but of the death of my maternal grandfather. And I was so much attached to him that his death appeared to be my own death.[2]

The deep love little Rajneesh felt for his grandfather was mutual. Rajneesh, the son of the old man's only child, experienced at first hand and in an overpowering way the death of his beloved grandfather. In his own words:

In the very first attack of death upon my grandfather, he lost his speech. For twenty-four hours we waited in the village for something to happen. However, there was no improvement. I remember a struggle on his part in an attempt to speak something but he could not speak. He wanted to tell something but could not tell it. Therefore, we had to take him toward the town in a bullock cart. Slowly, one after the other, his senses were giving way. He did not die all at once, but slowly and painfully. First his speech stopped, then his hearing. Then he closed his eyes as well. In the bullock cart I was watching everything closely and there was a long distance of thirty-two miles of travel.

Whatsoever was happening seemed beyond my understanding then. This was the first death witnessed by me and I did not even understand that he was dying. But slowly all his senses were giving way and he became unconscious. While we were nearby the town he was already half dead. His breathing still continued, but everything else was lost. After that he did not resume consciousness but, for three days, he continued breathing. He died unconsciously.

The slow losing of his senses and his final dying became very deeply engraved in my memory.[3]

It was as if Rajneesh's whole world fell apart with the disappearance of his beloved grandfather. Bhagwan continues to describe how he felt at his grandfather's death:

When he died I felt that it would be a betrayal to eat. Now I didn't want to live. It was childish, but through it something very deep happened. For three days I remained lying down. I would not come out of the bed. I said, "When he is dead, I do not want to live." I survived but these three days became a death experience. I died in a way and I came to realize (now I can tell about it though at that time, it was just a vague experience), I came to feel, that death is impossible. . . .[4]

When once asked what the event was that made him turn toward the spiritual, Bhagwan answered as follows:

There has been no such event. It happens many times that some event occurs and a person takes a turn in life. . . . In my life there has been no such event that can be singled out for causing such a change. . . . However, one memory in life which is worth remembering is that of death.[5]

It was the passing of his beloved grandfather that made him profoundly conscious of the phenomenon of death. So he says, "Death stared at me before the thrust of life began." Bhagwan adds further that, "For me the possibility of anyone else becoming my *center* was destroyed in the very first steps of my life. The first center that was formed broke down."[6] This death brought about a profound change in Rajneesh as an individual. It was as if a mold had come off and the real image had emerged out of it. The destruction of an intimate, deeply affectionate relationship brought with it the very freedom to be with one's self totally—to be alone. As Bhagwan puts it:

The "facticity" of aloneness took hold of me from the age of seven onwards. Aloneness became my nature. His death freed me forever from all relationships. His death became for me the death of all attachments. Thereafter I could not establish a bond of relationship with anyone. Whenever my relationship with anyone began to become intimate, that death stared at me.[7]

It must be understood that death did not make him negative to others, only that he stopped seeing others in the context of a binding relationship. From then on "death" became the context of every living being with whom he came into close contact. He remained conscious from then on that a person he might feel close to today could easily be gone tomorrow.

Reflecting further on his grandfather's death, Bhagwan says:

This event can be considered as the first which left a deep impact and influence on my mind. From that day onward, every day, every moment, the awareness of life invariably became associated with the awareness of death. From then onward, to be or not to be had the same value for me.[8]

The feeling of aloneness had significant implications for his natural growth. The very reality of death and the futility of seeking any permanent relationship brought him closer to the realization that in becoming alone one also becomes really happy. This is how Bhagwan explains it:

As that first feeling of aloneness became deeper and deeper, something new began to happen in [my] life. At first that aloneness had made me only unhappy, but slowly it began changing into happiness. . . . Thereafter, I did not suffer any unhappiness.[9]

It became apparent to him that his aloneness was, in fact, a state of becoming centered in his own self; it was a state in which he no longer felt dependent on the other. It was actually this freedom from dependence that made him permanently happy. He acknowledges that:

There was no other way but to revert back to my own self. I was, so to speak, thrown back to my own self. Slowly, that made me more and more happy. Afterwards I came to feel that this close observation of death at a tender age became a blessing in disguise for me.[10]

After the death of his grandfather, Rajneesh came to live with his parents and the family in Gadarwara. At this time, Gadarwara was a small town of about twenty thousand people—the population has since doubled. The town is about sixty miles from the city of Jabalpur. Its citizens are mainly grain and cloth merchants who follow the Hindu religion, and the town is surrounded by small farming villages. It has a primary school and a high school and a public library.

Rajneesh was admitted to the Gunj Primary School of Gadarwara at the age of seven. But even at this early age he found the traditional schooling too narrow and confining for his creative intelligence. For this reason he could not be persuaded for two years to begin his formal schooling regularly. His mother tells that in order to avoid going to school, he sometimes made up stories. Once he came home crying and said he would not go back to school because his teacher had given him physical punishment. His mother became upset and asked Rajneesh's youngest uncle, Shikharchand, to go and straighten out the teacher immediately. The uncle took young Rajneesh with him and headed for school. On the way, however, Rajneesh admitted to his uncle that he was pretending and that the teacher had not punished him. He simply did not enjoy going to school.

Rajneesh never could relate to dull and meaningless education and uncreative teachers. He rejected the whole system from the very beginning. He could not find anything worth learning, anything more than mere words or numbers or irrelevant details, anything to help in his inner search. This made him completely disinterested in following the normal course of schooling and created great aversion in him toward the subjects taught in school. Bhagwan describes his strong feelings in this matter:

From my childhood I was not interested in any subject that was taught in school—hence my poor history! I was always puzzled why these stupid names have to be remembered. Why, for what sin, are we punished to remember names of some people, dates, exact dates, exact names . . . ? And all these people have done is ugly! The history is bunk! Why should we be punished? So I was never present in the history class. I was never interested in language, any language.

My whole interest was, from the very beginning, how to transcend mind. Neither history can help, nor geography, nor mathematics, nor languages—nothing can help. All these things are irrelevant. My whole being was moving into a totally different direction.[11]

Rajneesh found it equally difficult to relate to any teacher because he could not find anyone who could understand his needs or who had experienced what he was searching for. This situation too, in a different way, threw Rajneesh back to his center—he once again found himself alone. "I could not accept anyone as my teacher," explains Bhagwan, "though I was always ready to be a student—but I was not finding anyone whom I might call 'my master.'" The phenomenon of death, which he had witnessed so intensely and closely, continued to remain an enigma, a deep mystery for him, and he was in search of someone who had realized what death was all about. "Everyone I found," continues Bhagwan, was very much involved in and with life. No one who had not seen death could ever become my teacher. I wanted to respect [them], but I could not. I could respect rivers, mountains and even stones, but not human beings. . . . I met no such teacher whom I could spontaneously respect, because I never felt that there was anything anyone knew that was such an absolute truth that without it life could have no meaning. . . . I had never felt that I was a small child and that I should remain under someone's protection and guidance. Not that I did not go to anyone: I did go to many people, but I always returned empty-handed and felt that all which was imparted I was also knowing. There was nothing which could be learned from them.[12]

This attitude created some difficulties for Rajneesh. Often he came to be seen, for example, as egotistical and immodest, discourteous and even seditious. Often he found himself in embarrassing moments. But there was another side to it also—and a very significant one. "I was thrown back upon myself from another direction as well," says Bhagwan, "because I never believed or felt that truth could be learned from others. There was only one way to learn—to learn from myself only."[13]

Right from the first grade Rajneesh became known for his beautiful handwriting and ability to paint. He began to read newspapers and magazines when he was in the second grade and became a member of the Gadarwara Public Library—the youngest person ever to be a member. While in elementary school, Rajneesh displayed his talent in writing poetry, short stories, articles, and in photography. In the sixth grade, Rajneesh edited a handwritten magazine, *Prayas,* meaning "effort."

One of the things that made young Rajneesh popular was his extraordinary storytelling ability, especially his narrating of detective stories. Swami Ageha Saraswati, a childhood friend, still remembers with fondness those days in school when, during the drawing class, after the assignment was over, Rajneesh would tell his fellow students sensational stories from detective novels.

The river that flows through Gadarwara and is called Shakkar (meaning "sugar," for its sweet water) played a very significant role in nourishing the body and soul of Rajneesh. He played in and with the river in all its moods. His whole being was involved with the river and its surroundings. Here is a very poetic description of his involvement with the river by Bhagwan himself:

In my childhood I used to go early in the morning to the river. It is a small village. The river is very, very lazy, as if not flowing at all. And in the morning when the sun is not yet arising, you cannot see whether it is flowing, it is so lazy and silent. And in the morning when nobody is there, the bathers have not yet come, it is tremendously silent. Even the birds are not singing in the morning—early, no sound, just a soundlessness pervades. And the smell of the mango trees hangs all over the river.

I used to go there, to the furthest corner of the river, just to sit, just to be there. There was no need to do anything, just being there was enough, it was such a beautiful experience to be there. I would take a bath, I would swim, and when the sun arose I would go to the other shore, to the vast expanse of sand, and dry myself there under the sun, and lie there, and sometimes even go to sleep.

When his mother asked what he did the whole morning, Rajneesh would say, "Nothing." Not satisfied, his mother pursued her question. Bhagwan says:

My mother would insist that I must have been doing something, so I would say, "Okay, I took a bath and I dried myself in the sun," and then she was satisfied. But I was not—because what happened there in the river is not expressed by the words: "I took a bath"; it looks so poor and pale. Playing in the river, floating in the river, swimming in the river, was such a deep experience that to say simply, "I took a bath," makes no sense of it; or to just say, "I went there, had a walk on the bank, sat there," conveys nothing.[14]

Rajneesh was fortunate in finding a person who was deeply in love with the river. This man gave young Rajneesh his first lessons in swimming—and he put him in touch with the river. The way this master swimmer taught him swimming gave young Rajneesh a very insightful experience into the secret of being total. This is how Bhagwan describes it:

In my childhood I was sent to a master swimmer. He was the best swimmer in town, and I have never come across a man who has been so tremendously in love with water. Water was god to him —he worshipped it—and the river was his home. Early—at three o'clock in the morning—you would find him on the river. In the evening you would find him on the river, and in the night you would find him sitting, meditating by the side of the river. His whole life consisted of being close to the river.

When I was brought to him—I wanted to learn how to swim— he looked at me, he felt something. He said, "But there is no way to learn how to swim. I can just throw you in the water and then swimming comes of its own accord. There is no way to learn it—it cannot be taught. It is a knack, not knowledge."

And that's what he did—he threw me in the water and he stood on the bank. Two or three times I went down and I felt that I was almost drowning. He was just standing there—he would not even try to help me! Of course, when your life is at stake, you do whatever you can. So I started throwing my hands about—it was haphazard, hectic, but the knack came. When life is at stake, you do whatever you can—and whenever you do whatever you can do totally, things happen!

I could swim! I was thrilled! "Next time," I said, "you need not throw me into it, I myself will jump. Now I know that there is a natural buoyancy of the body. It is not a question of swimming— it is only a question of getting in tune with the water element. Once you are in tune with the water element it protects you."[15]

Swami Ageha Saraswati relates the following river experiences from his childhood with Rajneesh:

It was a sheer joy to spend nights at the river with Bhagwan. It was the most incredible and sometimes frightening experience too because none of us, his friends, were ever sure what he would do while roaming on the banks. He was totally unpredictable, or to put it differently, he was utterly spontaneous, but we followed him with complete trust and the thrill of adventure.

We spent a good deal of our time with Bhagwan swimming in the river. Even with the river dangerously high, Bhagwan would ask us to jump in and swim across. Not only that, he would ask us to reach a specific spot on the other shore—we could never make it because the current and the flow of the river were so strong that we used to get swept miles away from the suggested spot. Bhagwan on the other hand would never fail even once in reaching the exact place he would have asked us to meet at.[16]

The river was also a place of refuge for Bhagwan. Whenever he felt deeply sad, he would come down to the river and sit in meditation. His friends have pointed out two occasions in particular—when his boyhood companion Shashi died, and again, on January 30, 1948, when Mahatma Gandhi was assassinated. Hearing the news of Gandhi's death, Rajneesh told his friends that he felt too sad to even weep. That evening he and his friends came to the river and sat in meditation.

For Rajneesh, the river and its surrounding environment was an ideal place to enter into deep meditation. Once, when asked whether he ever did any sadhana (spiritual practice), Bhagwan told a very interesting story. When the cinema was still new in Gadarwara, a show would last for four or five hours or even more, since the movie projector often broke down. Rajneesh would leave home early in the evening telling the family that he was going to the movies. He would in fact spend the rest of the evening lying naked in the sand on the river bank. The family did not mind his returning in the late hours, since they knew the situation at the movie theater.

Thus, his association with the river was more of an experiment in being in a state of complete and deep relaxation. It helped him experience the deeper levels of his consciousness.

As a child, Rajneesh's preoccupation with death was extraordinary. It was his common practice to follow people carrying a dead body to the cremation ground. When his parents asked him why he went to the cremation ground so often, to the funerals of strangers, he said: "The man is not my concern. Death—it is such a beautiful phenomenon, and one of the most mysterious. One should not miss it." Elaborating further on this, Bhagwan says: "So the moment I heard that somebody had died, I would be there, always watching, waiting, witnessing what was happening." He would watch and listen to people philosophizing over the death of the person and quoting from the scriptures. This kind of stupidity annoyed Rajneesh.

I started feeling "They are avoiding." By just becoming engaged in a discussion they are avoiding the phenomenon that is happening. They are not looking at the dead man. And the thing is there! Death is there and you are discussing it! What fools![17]

Swami Ageha Saraswati confirms that as a young boy Rajneesh would often go alone to the cremation ground and spend hours lying down there at night.

In view of this extraordinary tendency on the part of their son, the family again got worried about the prediction of Rajneesh's death, especially as he approached the age of fourteen. This time, too, Rajneesh survived physically, although he once again encountered death consciously. He told the family that if, according to the astrologer, death was certain, then it would be better if he was prepared for it. He wanted to meet death halfway; he wanted to encounter it consciously. The family was shocked and puzzled to hear this but did not interfere in his plans.

Rajneesh was determined to carry his plan out. He went to the school principal and requested a seven-day leave.

He told the principal that he was going to die. The principal could not believe his ears. Thinking that Rajneesh was planning to commit suicide, he asked for an explanation. Rajneesh told the principal about the astrologer's prediction regarding the possibility of his death in the fourteenth year. He also told the principal, "I am going into retreat for seven days to wait for death. If death comes, it is good to meet it consciously so that it becomes an experience."[18] The principal was astounded, but granted permission.

Rajneesh then went to an old, isolated temple in ruins near his village. A priest took care of the temple as well as he could. Rajneesh instructed the priest not to disturb him and asked the priest to provide him with something to eat and drink once a day while he lay in the temple waiting for death.

It was a beautiful experience for Rajneesh. Actual death never came, of course, but Rajneesh did almost everything possible "to become dead." He went through some strange and unusual feelings. Many things happened to him, but as Bhagwan says: "The basic note was this—that if you are feeling you are going to die, you become calm and silent."[19]

Some of his experiences were quite fascinating. Bhagwan narrates one relating to the fear of death as follows:

I was lying there. On the third or fourth day a snake entered the temple. It was in view; I was seeing the snake. But there was no fear. Suddenly I felt very strange. The snake was coming nearer and nearer and I felt very strange. There was no fear. So I thought, "When death is coming, it may be coming through this snake, so why be afraid? Wait!"

The snake crossed over me and went away. Fear had disappeared. If you accept death, there is no fear. If you cling to life, then every fear is there.[20]

Once death is accepted as a reality, its acceptance immediately creates a distance, a point from which one can observe the flow of events in life as an onlooker. This brings one above the pain, sorrow, worries and despair that usually accompany such events. Bhagwan describes his experience related to such a state of detachment:

Many times flies ... would fly around, they would creep over me, on my face. Sometimes I felt irritated and would have liked to throw them off but then I thought, "What is the use? Sooner or later I am going to die and then no one will be there to protect the body. So let them have their way."

The moment I decided to let them have their way, the irritation disappeared. They were still on the body but it was as if I was not concerned. They were as if moving, as if creeping on someone else's body. There was a distance immediately. If you accept death, a distance is created. Life moves far away with all its worries, irritations, everything. [21]

This is not to say that Bhagwan believed in the astrologer's prediction. Nevertheless, it did give him an opportunity, an incentive to explore it, to understand it experientially. Bhagwan concludes:

Physically some day I will die, of course. However, this prediction of the astrologer helped me very much because he made me aware very early about death. Continuously I could meditate and could accept that it was coming. [22]

Thus, in passing through the experience of being dead intensely and meditatively, it became quite apparent to Rajneesh that even though his body became dead in terms of its inability to respond to any stimuli, his consciousness remained fully aware. He reflects: "I died in a way, but I came to know that something deathless is there. Once you accept death totally, you become aware of it." [23]

Rajneesh also used the river for bringing him face to face with death. His uncles, friends, and relatives have mentioned how he would jump into the most dangerously flooding river and swim across it, or how he would climb up a seventy-foot-high bridge and from there jump into the flooding river. One of his most hair-raising experiments was diving into the whirlpool. For him falling into a whirlpool was "one of the most beautiful experiences." Bhagwan himself describes the nature of a whirlpool and his experience with it:

In rivers, particularly when they are flooded in the rains, many whirlpools are created, very powerful and strong. The water moves round and round like a screw. If you are caught in it, you will be forced, pulled toward the bottom and the deeper you go, the stronger the whirl becomes. The natural tendency of the ego is to fight with it, of course, because it looks like death and the ego is very much afraid of death. The ego tries to fight with the whirl and if you fight with it in a flooded river or near a waterfall where many whirls exist, you are lost because the whirl is very strong. You cannot fight with it.
   And this is the phenomenon of the whirl: on the surface the whirl is big; the deeper you go, the smaller and smaller the whirl becomes—stronger but smaller. And nearly at the bottom the whirl is so small you can simply get out of it with no fight. In fact, near the bottom, the whirl itself throws you out. But you have to wait for the bottom. If you are fighting on the surface, you are done for, you cannot survive. I have tried with many whirls; the experience is lovely.[24]

   This description illustrates Bhagwan's insight into death. The more one fights with death, the more one is bound to be twisted and engulfed by it; but if instead of resisting it, one allows oneself to go deeper into it meditatively, he or she is sure to come out with a tremendously thrilling experience. As one penetrates into its mysteries and reaches to the bottom of it, one automatically comes out of it unharmed and free of the fear of it.
   Whether swimming in the river or exploring other sources of adventure, Rajneesh remained the natural leader of a rather formidable gang of boys—they loved and respected him immensely. He was not only their comrade-in-arms, but also their mentor and guide. They were

amazed at the sharpness of his mind, his courage, and creative spirit. Rajneesh responded lovingly toward his friends and obviously cared for them. Not only did he himself experiment with new things, he encouraged his friends to do something new every day, to avoid repetition. He constantly reminded them to fight against superstition and hypocrisy.

Rajneesh and his gang became so well known in the town for their fearless escapades that even the local thieves and murderers, it is said by his friends, avoided confrontation with them. Their next target was anybody's guess. Their activities took place during the day, and even on full-moon nights. They would have fun liberating the donkeys of the town and riding them until the dawn.

Streams of complaints from indignant townsfolk reached Rajneesh's parents. His father, after hearing the stories about his prankster son, was rather perplexed as to what he could do, since most of the victims had nothing more to complain about than their own slightly wounded dignity. Generally, the father did not pay any attention, except on one occasion when in exasperation he locked his son in a toilet. He refused to let Rajneesh out until Rajneesh relented, but the punishment proved quite pointless because the son remained fully content to be left alone enjoying his own company. He remained locked in for hours without making any sound or movement. When the father enquired worriedly whether he was all right, Rajneesh told him in a cool voice that there was nothing to worry about and that he was happy to stay there indefinitely.

On a different occasion, a teacher punished Rajneesh for coming late to class by having him run around the school grounds. The young boy continued to come late and enjoy the exercise day after day until finally the teacher gave up the punishment.

Rajneesh's first rebellious act in school occurred when he was in the seventh grade. The principal was known for being a harsh disciplinarian who was especially strict in the observance of rules and regulations of the school. Rajneesh's free spirit never followed any imposed discipline—he believed in spontaneous self-discipline. At this school everyone was required to wear a cloth cap; Rajneesh was permitted, however, to wear the only woolen cap. But one day Rajneesh walked into the principal's room and declared calmly that henceforth the compulsory cloth cap would no longer be worn at the school—if cap wearing continued to be required, the students would go on strike. The principal must have read the situation correctly because from that day on caps were no longer required. Later Rajneesh led several other protests at the school against meaningless rules, harsh disciplines, and hypocritical behavior of teachers.

Rajneesh's rebelliousness also manifested itself in the form of pranks—whose purpose most often was to expose the hypocrites in society, to deflate their egos. His tricks and teasings were not malevolent, his intentions were never to hurt anyone; what he did was purely out of a good-natured sense of fun. On the surface his energy seemed to be directed at the person, but actually what he aimed at was age-old conditioning and ego-centered behavior. The person was never his target; it was the set pattern he was attacking. What Rajneesh did in the small setting of his hometown is the same kind of fun he has even now when he jibes at priests and the pope, pundits and politicians.

The nature and quality of Rajneesh's sense of humor can be seen in the following story told by his friend Swami Ageha Saraswati. In it one can see how he would enlist unsuspecting participants in his exploration of human behavior. It was his nature to take delight in exposing what he later called the "right victim."

There was a physician in Gadarwara who displayed a signboard with his name and a long list of his academic degrees. Rajneesh and his friends determined that when the doctor was in his office they would make it a point to read aloud his name and degrees from across the street. The gang followed Rajneesh's instructions: each time any one of them passed the doctor's office, he read the signboard aloud. When the doctor noticed it, he began to get annoyed—but the practice went on. The doctor became so annoyed about the situation that he made complaints to the parents of the youngsters. When the parents found out what was going on, they could see nothing offensive about it except that it was a little odd perhaps, and they felt rather amused by the whole thing. The story spread all over the little town and the doctor eventually recognized the egocentricity his sign symbolized. He quietly removed it.

Rajneesh was against the British domination of India. Another boyhood friend, Gulabbhai, shared his memories of Bhagwan, revealing young Rajneesh's deep concern over the political and social injustices in India. Gulabbhai was closely associated with Rajneesh from 1940 to 1950. Gulabbhai is nine years older than Bhagwan, and is also now a disciple. He runs a small business in Gadarwara.

"Living through insecurity, and fearlessness, were the outstanding qualities of Bhagwan," said Gulabbhai,

and we always marveled at the way he showed his courage in exposing the evils of the society. Even though Bhagwan was younger than some of us, we looked at him with awe and great respect. The kind of rebelliousness Bhagwan is showing now on such a wide scale, we witnessed on a smaller scale during our school days.[25]

According to Gulabbhai, Rajneesh never showed any interest in becoming politically involved—his main contribution was to speak out boldly against oppression, injustice, and hypocrisy. Even though he was strongly against the British rule, he never became a regular freedom fighter for the Congress Party or any other political party—his was always an independent voice.

Rajneesh admired Mahatma Gandhi for his sincerity and untiring efforts, but he was never impressed with Gandhi's ideas and idiosyncrasies. Later in the book we will examine Bhagwan's criticism of Gandhi.

However, in 1940, a representative of the Indian National Army (INA) led by Subhash Chandra Bose[26] met with Rajneesh and his uncle Shikharchand. He inspired them to form a youth branch of INA, and Rajneesh was made its captain. For some time Rajneesh was also a member of another nationalistic movement, Rashtriya Swayamsevak Sangh (RSS),[27] but did not stay in it for too long. In fact, he quit both INA and RSS because he could not accept any external discipline, ideology, or system.

Experimentation was as much a part of Rajneesh's life as his rebelliousness. Every day he did something new and different—the search continued on all levels. He experimented with sleep by arranging unusual hours for rising and going to bed; he tried fasting, eating at strange hours; he meditated standing in the river, in the woods, under the falling rain. He experimented with the occult and yogic breath control, with magic and telekinesis. He also experimented successfully with hypnosis.

"Often Rajneesh would involve his friends in his experiments," said another childhood friend of Bhagwan, Swami Sukhraj Bharati. For instance, describes Sukhraj, when they went boating Rajneesh would push a nonswimmer in the river, being careful to keep him from drowning, but at the same time allowing him to struggle. Sometimes he would push the head of a swimmer deep in the water for a few seconds. When the person forced himself out, Rajneesh would ask, "How was it?" By this he meant, how intense was the experience, how was it to be under water without being able to breathe? Rajneesh would then explain that it is only when one comes to a point of such tremendous intensity, where one's whole survival is at stake, that the real search for God begins.

Rajneesh's experiments included walking on a cliff in the middle of the night. His friend Swami Ageha Saraswati recalls:

He would take us in the middle of a dark night on a walk along the river. He would then invite us to climb upon the high hills and walk on the cliffs—it was a hair-raising experience. We were scared to death. Hundreds of feet below was the deep valley—one slip and we could have gone crashing down into pieces. Whenever he would take us on such adventures, we always knew, however, that his main intention was to have us experiment with fearlessness; his main purpose was to make us more and more aware, alert, and courageous.[28]

The experiments were directed toward the experience of the state of meditation. Bhagwan has described the walking on the cliff experiment and the experiment of jumping into the river from the bridge as examples of experiencing moments when one transcends the mind:

In my childhood days I used to take my friends to the river. There was a small path by the side of the river. To walk on that edge was very dangerous; just one step taken in unconsciousness and you will fall into the river, and that was the place where the river was the deepest. Nobody used to go there, but that was my most loved spot. And I would take all my friends to come along and to move with me on that narrow edge. Very few were ever ready to go along with me, but those few had really a beautiful experience. They would all report, "This is strange, how the mind stops!"

I would take my friends to the railway bridge to jump . . . into the river. It was dangerous . . . it was prohibited. There was always a policeman standing on the railway bridge because that was the place from where people used to commit suicide. We had to bribe the policeman [for allowing them to jump from the bridge]. And slowly, slowly he became aware that these are the same people—they don't die or anything . . . and they are not interested in suicide. In fact, he started loving us and stopped taking bribes. He said, "You can jump—I will not look at that side. Whenever you want you can come."

The bridge was very high and to jump from there ... And before you reached the river there was a time in the gap between the bridge and the river when the mind would suddenly stop.

Those were my first glimpses of meditation; that's how I became more and more interested in meditation. I started inquiring how these moments can be made available without going to the mountains, to the river, to the bridges; how one can allow oneself to move into these spaces without going anywhere, just by closing one's eyes. Once you have tasted it, it is not difficult.[29]

In all of these experiments, though, the main ingredient was courage. Bhagwan has, in fact, maintained all along that a seeker of Truth is one who is continuously experimenting and courage is necessary to experiment and to reach Truth. "Courage," according to Bhagwan, "is the greatest quality in life, because without courage there is no freedom, and without freedom no Truth. . . . "[30]

Rajneesh himself worked hard on remaining alert and aware. When he was in high school, for instance, one of the teachers Rajneesh loved and admired insisted that in answer to roll call students say "Present, Sir," and not "Yes, Sir." Commenting on this, Bhagwan says:

Now this was just whimsical. It doesn't matter whether you say, "Yes, Sir" or you say "Present, Sir." But I started feeling that he had some point in it, and I started meditating on it. And whenever he would call my name, I would say, "Present, Sir," and I would not [just] say it—I would feel it: "I am simply present, aware, alert." And I had beautiful moments; just for half a minute. I would become so present that the class would disappear, that the teacher would disappear.[31]

Rajneesh was equally alert to the conditioning imposed from outide. He says,

I was born in a Jaina family, and naturally, just as everybody else is conditioned, the conditioning was imposed on me. But I was continuously watchful, continuously alert; hence, I was not caught by the conditioning. And the conditioning is so subtle, once you are caught in it, you become incapable of thinking, seeing; anything that goes against your conditioning, you become deaf to it.[32]

Traditionally, Jains (or Jainas) do not eat meals after sunset. Rajneesh was brought up in this tradition and its conditioning once caused him an awful experience. Bhagwan recounts the following incident:

Up to my eighteenth year, I had not eaten in the night. Then I went with my few friends to see a fort, far away in the jungles. They were all Hindus, and the fort was such a beauty that the whole day they were not interested in preparing food. I was the only Jaina, and I could not insist, because thirty people were not interested in cooking food in the day. So I kept quiet. In the night they cooked food. Now, the whole day's wandering in the forest, in the ruins of that old ancient castle: I was tired, hungry. I had never known such hunger. But my eighteen years' conditioning: You cannot eat in the night.

And then they started preparing beautiful food, and the smell of the food and so close by . . . And they all started persuading me, and they said, "Nobody is here, and nobody will tell to your family, to your parents; nobody will ever know." I resisted—but the more I resisted, the more I was tempted. Finally I yielded; I ate. The food was delicious. But the whole night I suffered hell. I vomited at least seven times. That eighteen years of conditioning was not an easy thing to get rid of. I could not digest that food; my whole body revolted. Unless the whole food was thrown out, I could not sleep. . . .[33]

Rajneesh exhibited the ability to think rationally and to articulate his ideas logically and effectively from a very early age. He began giving speeches and participating in debates in the sixth grade. This activity increased from the ninth grade onward. Swami Ageha Saraswati, his friend, told me that Rajneesh—even in those early days—was known for his ability to pick any side in a debate and defeat the opponent in the argument. He was once awarded a first prize in a debating contest in which he spoke in favor of Jawaharlal Nehru's foreign policy of "non-alignment." He also once gave a series of seven-day talks on religion and spirituality at a friend's house. Even as an adolescent he was occasionally invited to enter into open debate with well-known scholars, priests, and pundits. With his scathing tongue and pointed questions, he always made them uncomfortable, but forthrightness and open-minded searching remained his outstanding qualities. An illustration of this can be seen in a speech he gave when he spoke at Teachers' Day at D. N. Jain High School in Jabalpur. Teachers' Day is observed in India on September 5, the birthday of the former president of India, professor and philosopher S. Radhakrishnan. Rajneesh shocked the audience when he spoke the following words:

Today is the most unfortunate day for teachers. . . . This day is being observed just because S. Radhakrishnan was once a teacher and is now the president. The real honor for the teachers will be when the president would give up his presidency and become a teacher.[34]

His passionate search made him explore books on every possible subject. Often he read all night, which occasionally gave him a headache, but he would apply a pain-killing balm to his forehead and continue reading. Then at dawn he would go to the river and take a swim. Although as a young boy he played games such as field hockey, soccer, and volleyball, he was more interested in reading. Many of the books at the Gadarwara Public Library still have cards that show only Rajneesh's signature. The books ranged from politics and philosophy to science, religion to detective novels. Not only did he himself read widely, but he insisted that his friends also read something other than the usual textbooks. The Indian Nobel Laureate in literature, Rabindranath Tagore, was one of his favorite authors.

Because of his extraordinary reading habits, Rajneesh

rarely attended school. Not only that, he was branded a communist, for he read extensively in Marx and Engels and other communist literature, and was threatened with expulsion from school. His interest in communism during high school stemmed from his deep concern for the poor. With the help of his friends, he built a small library that contained mostly communist literature. Their adolescent concern for the poor extended to fantasies about becoming Robin Hood and his merry men. It is said that they planned to buy guns and obtain a license from the police to use them in order to force the rich to give to the poor. But the plan did not, of course, go through. Rajneesh, according to his uncle Amritlal, even formed a group of young people that regularly discussed communist ideology and their opposition to religion. Amritlal had seen written on the walls of their meeting place: "Religion is an opium."

Despite his serious interest in communist thinking, Rajneesh personally leaned toward socialism. He and his friends believed socialism was the answer to the economic plight of India. During this period in his life, Rajneesh remained an atheist, openly critical of religious rituals and blind faith in the scriptures. (It must be emphasized here, however, that the meditations Rajneesh practiced were not part of any religious ritual, or prescribed by any religion. In Bhagwan's view, meditation is essentially a secular phenomenon; it has nothing to do with following a religion. We shall hear more of his views on meditation in Chapter 5.) Bhagwan describes his attitude those days in the following words:

But the truth is that those who had known me from my childhood would never have believed that religion and I could ever go together. It was beyond their expectations because what they were calling or knowing as religion I had always fought against. What they were calling worship was just so much nonsense for me. What they called a sannyasin was for me nothing but an escapist. What they called scriptures, to which they used to bow their heads in worship, were but ordinary books for me upon which I could rest my foot. Whatsoever they asserted as being beyond doubt, I dragged into uncertainty and suspicion. Their God, their soul, and their salvation were all matters of joke and fun for me.[35]

Although Rajneesh continued to remain interested in socialism while still in high school, he became more and more critical of it. In fact, around 1950, his friend Gulabbhai reports, he began criticizing eminent leaders of the Indian Socialist Party such as Jaya Prakash Narayan. Rajneesh once even attended the national executive meeting of the Socialist Party, which was held at Panchmarhi,[36] as an observer. The meeting proved quite disappointing.

And yet, regardless of Rajneesh's reading of Marx and socialist literature or his participation in organizations, his search remained exclusively spiritual. The spiritual quest continued to be the undercurrent in all his activities. It appears that his disillusionment with Marx and socialistic ideas made him think with greater clarity about his own sense of direction and commitment. It became quite apparent to him that the roots of human misery and unhappiness were not hidden in any particular social or political system. Rather, their origin was somewhere else. Rajneesh came to see that only a revolution in consciousness, not politics, can bring peace and happiness. Another longtime friend of Bhagwan, Shyam Soni, recalls:

Once, when we were in high school, on a full moon night, some of us were sitting on the bank of the river. It was around eleven o'clock, and everything was so quiet and peaceful. Suddenly, Rajneesh broke the silence and said that he had a role to play in the field of religion—nowhere else. His place was in religion. I liked and appreciated his feeling, but could not believe it, because in those days he was very much into communism. I did not have to wait too long, however, since I began to notice soon after that night how everything except religion had become totally insignificant to him.[37]

This transition in Rajneesh from interest in communism and socialism to religion and spirituality took place between 1945 and 1950.

Despite his outside activities and his preoccupation with ideas, he remained very loving and respectful toward his family members. He did not, however, hesitate to express his views frankly when necessary and always remained firm in his decisions. The following incident between Rajneesh and his father illustrates the point.

When Rajneesh was young, he was very fond of wearing long hair, so much so that the customers would often ask his father, Dadda, whether Rajneesh was a boy or a girl. It always bothered Dadda to keep explaining that Rajneesh was indeed a boy. The customers were always astonished at seeing a boy with such long hair. Dadda finally asked Rajneesh to get a haircut; when he refused, the father slapped Rajneesh—though not too hard. That was the first time Dadda had ever slapped Rajneesh and afterward he felt so bad he apologized to him. Nevertheless, Rajneesh left immediately and got his head shaved. Seeing his shaven head Dadda was shocked, because according to the Indian custom, a son is supposed to shave his head only on his father's death. Rajneesh told Dadda to make a choice, either he would grow his hair or keep his head shaved. Dadda let him grow his hair; at least it stopped giving people the impression that he was dead![38] Thereafter, it became clear to Dadda that he could not impose his will upon his son.

At sixteen, Rajneesh received yet another deep shock when his girlfriend from childhood, Shashi, died of typhoid. She lived near the same old temple where Rajneesh had "died" at fourteen. She was a couple of years younger than Rajneesh and her father was a medical doctor. Shashi was very deeply in love with Rajneesh. Whenever Rajneesh came for meditation at the temple, she would watch him from her garden or window. Often she would follow him to the temple, which sometimes annoyed the young man for he usually wanted to be left alone. Rajneesh would ask one of his friends to guard the temple door so that Shashi would not disturb him in meditation. Despite this, Shashi knew that Rajneesh returned her love. He affectionately called her Gudiya and lovingly accepted the food she brought to him after his meditation.

When Shashi was on her deathbed, Rajneesh was with her. Death was certain, but so was Shashi's determination to return, to be with her beloved and to take care of him. She promised him she would come back. He, too, promised her that he would call her, bring her back. She also made him promise that he would never accept another woman, that he would not get married. She did not want to leave him—she never wanted to leave him.[39]

One of Bhagwan's closest friends told me that, after Shashi's death, Rajneesh became even more distant and detached; for many days he did not talk to anybody. "I do not remember," Bhagwan says,

whether I ever cultivated any friendship, though there were many who wanted to be my friends. Many persons made friends with me, and they enjoyed making friends with me because it was not possible to make me an enemy. But I do not recall that I have ever gone to anyone of my own accord in order to make a friend. It is not that I never welcomed friendship. If someone made a friend of me, I wholeheartedly welcomed it. But even then I could not become a friend in the ordinary sense; I have always remained aloof.

This kept him free, in a way, to be himself.

Neither with any of my teachers, nor with any fellow students, nor with any other, could I develop such a relationship as would drown me or break my being an island. Friends came and . . . stayed with me. I met many people as well; I had many friends. But from my side there was nothing that could make me dependent upon them or which would cause me to remember them. . . . I may live with everyone, but whether I am in a crowd or a society, with a friend or an intimate, I am still alone. Nothing touches me; I remain untouched.[40]

The loneliness that seized Rajneesh's consciousness, right from the time his grandfather died, was essentially a state of aloneness, a state of self-fulfillment; it had a very positive quality. "The cause of unhappiness lies in our attaching ourselves to the other," explains Bhagwan,

in expectation from the other, in the hope of gaining happiness from the other. You never actually gain happiness, but the hope is always sustained. And whenever that hope gives way, frustration begins. Thus, in the very first experience [his grandfather's death], I became so badly disappointed from the other that I did not try again . . . thereafter, I never became unhappy. Then a new type of happiness began to be experienced which can never come from the other.[41]

Rajneesh derived a deeply spiritual insight from his encounters with death. Finding it futile to seek happiness from the other, he was forced, from an early age, to encounter his self from where he touched upon spiritual reality. It became quite apparent to him that:

When encountering oneself, unhappiness is experienced in the beginning, but authentic happiness progressively comes about as the encounter continues. On the contrary, encountering the other gives happiness in the beginning, but unhappiness in the end. So being thrown upon oneself, in my view, begins the journey toward the spiritual.[42]

So from a very early age Bhagwan used every experience, every situation, as a stepping stone toward inner growth. His awareness kept him open to learning from experience and not missing any opportunity in his search for Truth. The deaths of his sister, his grandfather, and Shashi gave him extraordinary chances to understand the limitations created by attachment with the other and, hence, to transcend the duality. He seized upon these chances and made himself really free to be by himself. Bhagwan's own observation in this regard is important:

Life gives many opportunities for being thrown back to oneself. But the more clever we are, the quicker we are in rescuing ourselves from such an opportunity. At such moments we move out from ourselves. If my wife dies, I am immediately in search, and then I marry another. If my friend is lost, I begin to search for another. I cannot leave any gap. By filling that gap, the opportunity I would have had to revert back to my own self is lost in a moment, along with its immense possibilities.

If I had become interested in the other, I would have lost the opportunity to journey toward the Self.[43]

In experiencing his aloneness, Rajneesh became more of an "outsider," a "stranger." He became rooted in a state of detachment in which even in the midst of activities and people, he remained unidentified, an outsider. "I became a universe unto myself," says Bhagwan. Referring to his grandfather's death, he says:

This new experience—and a strange one at that—gave me a sort of pain, although it was a "joyous pain." It was like this: that at that young age I began to feel and experience a sort of maturity and elderliness. In this experience there was no ego involvement, but an individuality was still there. . . .[44]

It is not too difficult to see that in his childhood and adolescence Rajneesh lived a very eventful and independent life. Whatever he did he took full interest in and was honest about. Significantly, however, he never identified himself with an act; he always maintained a distance between the act and himself. Throughout his adventures, and in each of his experiments, he never let himself be led astray by unawareness.

His actions were part of his continuous search of that which is eternal, the ultimate in experience. The story in the next chapter shows how this search reached an intensity that brought him enlightenment.

4.

Enlightenment

In 1951, after graduating from high school in Gadar-wara at the age of nineteen, Rajneesh went to Jabalpur, where he enrolled at Hitkarini College. He lived with his cousins Kranti and Arvind, who were about his age. Kranti and Arvind were the children of one of Bhagwan's father's sisters, Ratnibai. Ratnibai died when they were young and their father remarried so they were brought up by their aunt Makhmalbai and her husband, Kundanlal Samaiya, who had no children of their own.

Kranti was married at a very young age, but unfortunately her husband died just one year after the marriage. Rajneesh felt very deeply for his widowed cousin and helped her as much as he could, encouraging her to pursue her education. She later became a school teacher. Arvind graduated from a business school and became a college professor. As long as Rajneesh was in Jabalpur, all three stayed together. They earned enough, supported each other, and lived a comfortable life.

Rajneesh continued to do in college what he had done in high school: he remained as uncompromising, unconventional, and forthright as ever. He willingly accepted whatever the consequences were for exercising his freedom. It did not take too long for him to get into trouble. Two years after he entered college he was on his way out.

Rajneesh was particularly troublesome in his classes in philosophy and logic. No matter what the professor said, Rajneesh would invariably question it and start a long but logical argument, so that the professor never got very far in covering the coursework. When admonished by the professor not to argue, Rajneesh pointed out that this would defeat the whole purpose of being in a class on philosophy and logic. His questions and arguments, based on his keen sense of inquiry, pertained strictly to the prescribed coursework. But finally the professor could take it no more and delivered an ultimatum to the principal: "Either Rajneesh goes or I go." The principal called Rajneesh into his office and asked him to leave the college. He admitted that Rajneesh was not really at fault, but he could not see one of his most senior and well-respected professors resign.

Rajneesh understood the situation and agreed to leave, provided that the principal took the responsibility for gaining admission for Rajneesh at another college—a difficult demand, since the school year was almost at an end. The principal agreed to make contacts. Rajneesh's reputation had already traveled all over town and other colleges were reluctant to admit him. Finally, the principal of D. N. Jain College of Jabalpur agreed to admit Rajneesh, but on the condition that he not question professors as he had before. Rajneesh said that was impossible, that it would be better if he stayed home instead of attending class. The principal allowed him to stay home and bent the attendance rules so that Rajneesh was allowed to appear only for examinations. Rajneesh used this free time to find a job at the daily newspaper as assistant editor. He stayed with the newspaper for only a few months.

However, this period was not particularly significant for either Rajneesh's employment or his education. Rather, it was important because of the extraordinary intensity of his personal search for the eternal. This was the most critical time of his life. He was beset with doubts and feelings of terrible insecurity and emptiness. The situation was all the more painful because there was no one to guide him, to empathize with him—he was without a master, he was alone on the path.

As has been mentioned before, Rajneesh would not accept anything without questioning. He was especially unwilling to accept anything about the existence of God without encountering that reality face-to-face, without personal experience of it. He questioned all, he rejected all—including enlightened beings such as Krishna, Mahavir, Buddha, and Jesus, and scriptures such as the Vedas, Upanishads, Bible, and Koran. Thus, now that he realized these sources could no longer help him, his search became fully personal and solitary and he almost went mad. In Bhagwan's words:

In every small matter, there was doubt and nothing but doubt. . . . Questions remained without any answer. In one respect, I was as good as mad. I was myself afraid that anytime I might become mad. I was not able to sleep at night.

Throughout the night and day . . . questions hovered around me. . . . I was in a deep sea, so to speak, without any boat or bank anywhere. Whatever boats had been there, I had myself sunk or denied. There were many boats and many sailors, but I had . . . refused to step into anyone else's boat. I felt that it was better to drown by oneself . . . than to step into someone else's boat. If this was where life was to lead me, to drowning myself, then I felt that this drowning should be accepted.

My condition was one of utter darkness. It was as if I had fallen into a deep dark well. In those days I had many times dreamt that I was falling and falling and going deeper into a bottomless well. And many times I . . . awakened from a dream full of perspiration, sweating profusely, because the falling was endless without any ground or place anywhere to rest my feet . . . for me there was no clear path. It was all darkness. Every next step for me was in darkness—aimless and ambiguous. My condition was full of tension, insecurity and danger.[1]

There was no escape, there were no shortcuts for Rajneesh. He knew full well that he was facing a very crucial time in his life: with a little bit of unawareness or loss of patience, or lack of courage, he could go berserk. Again, the absence of a master is what made this situation so critical. He searched long and hard, but he could not find one. "It is very rare to find a master," he confides,

rare to find a being who has become a non-being, rare to find a presence who is almost an absence, rare to find a man who is simply a door to the divine, an open door to the divine which will not hinder you, through which you can pass. It is very difficult. . . . Yes, sometimes it happens that a person has to work without a Master. If the Master is not available, then one has to work without a Master, but then the journey is very hazardous.[2]

This tremendously intense and challenging situation lasted for one whole year. It put Rajneesh into a most difficult state of mind. Bhagwan gives a description of what he went through during this period:

For one year it was almost impossible to know what was happening . . . Just to keep myself alive was a very difficult thing, because all appetite disappeared. Days would pass and I would not feel any hunger, days would pass and I would not feel any thirst. I had to force myself to eat, force myself to drink. The body was so non-existential that I had to hurt myself to feel that I was still in the body. I had to knock my head against the wall to feel whether my head was still there or not. Only when it hurt would I be a little in the body.

Every morning and every evening I would run for five to eight miles. People used to think that I was mad. Why was I running so much? Sixteen miles a day! It was just to feel myself . . . not to lose contact with myself . . . I could not talk to anybody because everything had become so inconsistent that even to formulate one sentence was difficult. In the middle of the sentence I would forget what I was saying; in the middle of the way I would forget where I was going. Then I would have to come back . . .

I had to keep myself shut [up] in my room. I made it a point not to talk, not to say anything, because to say anything was to say that I was mad.

For one year it persisted. I would simply lie on the floor and look at the ceiling and count from one to a hundred then back from a hundred to one. Just to remain capable of counting was at least something. Again and again I would forget. It took one year for me to gain a focus again, to have a perspective.

There was nobody to support me; there was nobody to say where I was going and what was happening. In fact, everybody was against . . . my teachers, my friends, my well wishers.[3]

During these enormously difficult times, Kranti took great care of Rajneesh and looked after his needs with love and dedication. Rajneesh often complained of severe headaches which caused her great worry. She and her brother Arvind wanted very much to do something, to find some cure for Rajneesh's painful headaches, but he would tell them lovingly not to bother since there was nothing anybody could do about it.

Bhagwan's father also mentioned Bhagwan's headaches. Once the pain became so severe that Kranti and Arvind sent an urgent message to Gadarwara, and Dadda had to rush to Jabalpur. Dadda thought that the headaches were caused by the heavy reading Rajneesh used to do. He remembered how, when in Gadarwara, Rajneesh simply kept applying the pain-killing balm to his forehead and continued to read. Bhagwan's mother also recalled an earlier incident when Rajneesh once had an excruciating pain in his head and blood starting running from his nose. She got worried, but fortunately, after a while, the bleeding stopped. But the headaches of these early years of college did not seem to be related to his reading habits. Rather, they were due to the psychological state Rajneesh was passing through.

Looking at his physical and psychological condition, the family began to suspect that the astrologer's prediction of

Rajneesh's death at twenty-one might come true. They took him from one doctor to another. Rajneesh alone knew that these frantic efforts were meaningless. He insisted that there was no need to see a doctor, since no medicine would do him any good. Bhagwan describes one remarkable visit to a physician: .

I was also taken to a *vaidya,* to a physician. In fact, I was taken to many doctors and to many physicians but only one Ayurvedic[4] *vaidya* told my father, "He is not ill. Don't waste your time." Of course, they were dragging me from one place to another. And many people would give me medicines and I would tell my father, "Why are you worried? I am perfectly okay." But nobody would believe what I was saying. They would say, "You keep quiet. You just take the medicine. What is wrong in it?" So I used to take all sorts of medicines.

There was only one *vaidya* who was a man of insight. His name was Pundit Bhagirath Prasad. . . . That old man is gone, but he was a rare man of insight. He looked at me and he said, "He is not ill." And he started crying and said, "I have been searching for this state myself. He is fortunate. In this life I have missed this state. Don't take him to anybody. He is reaching home." And he cried tears of happiness.

He became my protector—my protector against the doctors and other physicians. He said to my father, "You leave it to me. I will take care." He never gave me any medicine. When my father insisted, he just gave me sugar pills and told me, "These are sugar pills. Just to console them, you can take them. They will not harm, they will not help. In fact, there is no help possible."[5]

The physician's reading of Rajneesh's condition was correct because his disease was unusual; he was not an ordinary patient. Rajneesh knew his condition and its causes better than any medical practitioner.

Now it was beyond me, it was happening. I had done something. Unknowingly, I had knocked at the door. Now the door had opened. I had been meditating for many years, just sitting silently doing nothing, and by and by I started getting into that space, that heart space, where you are and you are not doing anything; you are simply there, a presence, a watcher.[6]

The intensity of Rajneesh's meditations continued to deepen. His experiences were leading him toward the big explosion. Of all the meditations he used to do, the one that involved sitting in the top of a tree turned out to be particularly powerful. This fascinating experience occurred at Saugar, in Madhya Pradesh, approximately one year before the big event took place. While studying in college at Jabalpur, Rajneesh was invited to participate in a debating contest sponsored by Saugar University. Rajneesh was there for three days, and he describes what happened:

I used to sit on a tree and meditate in the night. Many times I felt that when I meditated sitting on the earth, my body became powerful and had the upper hand—perhaps because the body is made out of earth. The talk about the yogis going to the mountaintops or the heights of the Himalayas is certainly not vain, but is definitely based on scientific principles. The greater the distance between the body and the earth, the more the physical force or pressure of the body lessens . . . and the power of the inner force increases. That is why I used to climb up a tall tree and get myself engrossed in meditation for hours every night.

One night I got so lost in meditation that I did not know when my body fell down from the tree. I looked about askance when I saw my body lying on the ground. I was surprised at this happening. How it happened that I was sitting on the tree and my body was lying on the ground I could not understand at all. It was a very queer experience. A bright line, a glittering silver cord from the navel of my body was joined on to me up above where I was perched on the tree. It was beyond my capacity to understand or foresee what would happen next and I worried [about] how I would return to my body. How long that trance lasted I do not know, but that unique experience was not known to me before.

That day for the first time, I saw my own body from outside, and since that day the mere physical existence of my body finished forever. And from that day death also ceased to exist, because that day I experienced that the body and spirit are two different things, quite separate from each other. That was the most important moment: my realization of the spirit that is within every human body.

It is really very difficult to say how long that experience lasted. As morning dawned, two women carrying milk cans from some nearby village passed by that way and saw my body . . . lying there. I saw them looking at my body from the top of the tree where I was sitting. They came near the body and sat there beside it. They touched my forehead with their palms and in a moment, as if by sheer force of attraction, I returned inside my body and my eyes opened.

I felt that a woman can create a charge of electricity in the body of a man and similarly a man can too in the body of a woman. Then I pondered over the coincidence of the woman's touch to my forehead and my instant return to my body. How and why did all that happen? Many more experiences of this sort occurred to me and I understood why in India those spiritualists who carried on experiments on *samadhi* [an uninterrupted state of pure consciousness][7] and the fact of death got women to collaborate with them. If in a deep and profound *samadhi* the spiritual *self, tejas sharira,* has gone out of the man's physical body, it cannot return to the body without the cooperation and assistance of a woman. In the same way if it has gone out of a woman's body, it cannot return without the assistance of a man. No sooner do the bodies of a man and woman come in contact than a current is established and an electrical circle is completed, and that very instant the consciousness of the spirit which has gone out returns.

Thereafter I experienced this phenomenon six times within the period of six months. During those eventful six months, I felt that my life span became less by ten years: that is to say, if I was to live seventy years, now with these experiences I would only live a life of sixty years. Such extraordinary experiences I had in those six months! The hair on my chest turned white and I failed to grasp the meaning of all those happenings. Then I thought, and I realized that whatever connection or link there was between this physical body and that spiritual being was interrupted and the adjustment that existed naturally between them was broken.[8]

As Rajneesh entered deeper and deeper into the mysteries of meditation, his questions disappeared. His *doing* ceased; the search came to a point from which there was nowhere to go. As had happened years ago at the time of his grandfather's death, Rajneesh was brought to his center —but now it was forever. Bhagwan recounts that deep down there was emptiness, there was no doer. He had lost ambition; he did not have any desire to become anybody, or to reach anywhere. He did not care for God or for *nirvana*. "The Buddha-disease had completely disappeared," says Bhagwan.[9]

The opportune moment had come. The doors were about to open, the dawn was not too far. In Bhagwan's words:

One day a questionless condition came about. It is not that I received the answer—no! Rather, all the questions just fell away and a great void was created. This was an explosive situation. Living in that condition was as good as dying. And then the person died who had been asking questions. After that experience of void, I asked no questions. All matters on which questions could be asked became non-existent. Previously, there was only asking and asking. Thereafter, nothing like questioning remained.[10]

Bhagwan himself did not reveal the event of enlightenment to anyone for about twenty years. The story came out rather dramatically one night while Bhagwan was living in the Woodland Apartments in Bombay. Kranti, Bhagwan's cousin, was often asked by friends if she knew when Bhagwan was enlightened. She could not tell them because she did not know, but every time someone new asked her about it, she again felt the impulse to try to find out from Bhagwan.

Kranti finally asked Bhagwan about his enlightenment:

Last night, November 27, 1972, the curiosity that I had carried for so long became uncontrollable. It was about eleven thirty.

After taking his milk Bhagwan had gone to bed. I also lay down in my bed and suddenly I felt like asking Bhagwan when he had attained enlightenment. No sooner had the thought occurred to me than I asked, "When did you attain enlightenment?" Bhagwan laughed and said, "Do you yourself feel inspired to know about it or is it because people keep on asking you?"

I said, "Both things are true, please tell me." Bhagwan started laughing again and said, "I'll tell you some other time." I said, "I want to know right now." He said, "Start thinking and you will come to know."

I remained quiet for a while. Then I said, "I think you attained enlightenment at the age of twenty-one or twenty-two when you were studying in Inter [Intermediate: second year of college]. No sooner had I mentioned this than Bhagwan said a little seriously, "At the age of twenty-one, not twenty-two." Then I became curious about the date and the year and asked about it.

Bhagwan Shree said, "On March 21, 1953." After some quiet, I asked again, "Where did it happen? Did anything unusual take place on that day?"

Bhagwan said, "Try to recall, you will come to remember everything." I kept lying silently, and remembered a night twenty years ago. I said, "That night when all of a sudden at twelve o'clock you told me you were leaving, and then returned at three o'clock."

Bhagwan Shree said, "You got it exactly right, precisely on that night." I could not believe that what I was seeing was really true. And here was Bhagwan telling me that it was indeed true. Could I see in the past? It was all his play. It was all his doing. While such thoughts were clamoring in my mind, yet another curiosity arose: At what time in the night, where and at which place did Bhagwan Shree become enlightened? I immediately asked, "Where did you go that night?"

Bhagwan said, "To the Bhanvartal Garden." No sooner had he said, "to the garden" than I remembered a tree. I said, "You went to the garden and sat under the ashoka tree."

He said, "No, I was under the maulshree." Then I asked, "Since you were in the garden between twelve and three, at what time in the night did the event take place?"

He said, "Recall and you will remember it." I was quiet for a while and all the scenes of that evening began to appear before my eyes: how he left home, how he woke me up gently and said he was going out, didn't know when he would return. He left just after telling me that much, while I stayed up the whole night waiting for his return.

Then the whole event began to reveal itself to me. I could even recall his *mudra* [body posture]. Somehow I felt that the event must have taken place at two o'clock. As I got the idea of two o'clock, I told Bhagwan about it.

He said, "It happened exactly at two o'clock. Now you are catching it all right." Once again I was full of amazement, but I was so filled with joy that it became impossible to sleep. Again and again I felt like waking up everyone and telling them what I had learned.[11]

Bhagwan himself gives the reason for not revealing the story of his enlightenment for almost twenty years as follows:

Many people have asked me that if I became enlightened in 1953, why did I keep silent? For almost twenty years I never said anything about it to anybody unless somebody suspected himself, unless somebody asked me on his own. . . . "We feel that something has happened to you. We don't know what it is, but one thing is certain: that something has happened, you are no more the same as we are and you are hiding it."

In those twenty years not more than ten people had asked me, and even then I avoided them as much as I could, unless I felt that their desire was genuine. And I told them only when they had promised to keep it a secret. And they all fulfilled it. Now they are all sannyasins. . . . I said, "You wait, you wait for the right moment; only then I will declare it."

I have learned much from the past Buddhas. If Jesus had kept quieter about his being the son of God it would have been far more beneficial to humanity.

Bhagwan had made it a point not to reveal it unless he stopped traveling about the country, for to have it known would mean great risk to his life.

For twenty years continuously I was moving, and there was not a single bodyguard. And I was in constant danger: stones were being thrown at me, shoes were being thrown at me.

I would reach a town after traveling twenty-four hours in the train, and the crowd wouldn't allow me to get down into the station; they would force me to go back. There would ensue a fight between those who wanted me to get down from the train and those who did not want me to get down, in their town at least.

If I had declared that I was enlightened, I would have been killed very easily; there was no problem in it; it would have been so simple. But for twenty years I kept absolutely silent about it. I declared it only when I saw that I had gathered enough people who would understand it . . . enough people who were mine, who belonged to me. I declared it only when I knew that I could create my own small world and I was no more concerned with the crowds and the masses and the stupid mob.[12]

After over twenty years, Bhagwan described in his own words that incredibly powerful experience. He has articulated the experience in more detail than any other enlightened being, any Buddha has ever done before:

I am reminded of the fateful day of March 21, 1953. For many lives I had been working—working upon myself, struggling, doing whatsoever can be done—and nothing was happening.

Now I understand why nothing was happening. The very effort was the barrier, the very ladder was preventing, the very urge to seek was the obstacle. Not that one can reach without seeking. Seeking is needed, but then comes a point when seeking has to be dropped. The boat is needed to cross the river but then comes a moment when you have to get out of the boat and forget all about it and leave it behind. Effort is needed, without effort nothing is possible. And also with only effort, nothing is possible.

Just before twenty-first March, 1953, seven days before, I stopped working on myself. A moment comes when you see the whole futility of effort. You have done all that you can do and nothing is happening. You have done all that is humanly possible. Then what else can you do? In sheer helplessness one drops all search.

And the day the search stopped, the day I was not seeking for something, the day I was not expecting something to happen, it started happening. A new energy arose, out of nowhere. It was not coming from any source. It was coming from nowhere and everywhere. It was in the trees and in the rocks and the sky and the sun and the air—it was everywhere. And I was seeking so hard, and I was thinking it is very far away. And it was so near and so close.

. . . Seven days I lived in a very hopeless and helpless state, but at the same time something was arising. When I say hopeless I don't mean what you mean by the word hopeless. I simply mean there was no hope in me. Hope was absent. I am not saying that I was hopeless and sad. I was happy in fact, I was very tranquil, calm and collected and centered. Hopeless, but in a totally new meaning. There was no hope, so how could there be hopelessness. Both had disappeared.

The hopelessness was absolute and total. Hope had disappeared and with it its counterpart, hopelessness, had also disappeared. It was a totally new experience—of being without hope. It was not a negative state. . . . It was absolutely positive. It was not just absence, a presence was felt. Something was overflowing in me, overflooding me.

And when I say I was helpless, I don't mean the word in the dictionary sense. I simply say I was selfless. That's what I mean when I say helpless. I have recognized the fact that I am not, so I cannot depend on myself, so I cannot stand on my own ground. . . . I was in . . . a bottomless abyss. But there was no fear, because there was nothing to protect. There was no fear, because there was nobody to be afraid.

Those seven days were of tremendous transformation, total transformation. And the last day the presence of a totally new energy, a new light and new delight, became so intense that it was almost unbearable, as if I was exploding, as if I was going mad with blissfulness. The new generation in the West has the right word for it: I was blissed out, stoned.

It was impossible to make any sense out of . . . what was happening. It was a very non-sense world—difficult to figure it out, difficult to manage in categories, difficult to use words, languages, explanations. All scriptures appeared dead and all the words that have been used for this experience looked very pale, anemic. This was so alive. It was like a tidal wave of bliss.

The whole day was strange, stunning, and it was a shattering experience. The past was disappearing, as if it had never belonged to me, as if I had read about it somewhere, as if I had dreamed about it, as if it was somebody else's story I have heard and somebody told it to me. I was becoming loose from my past, I was being uprooted from my history, I was losing my autobiography. I was becoming a non-being, what Buddha calls *anatta*. Boundaries were disappearing, distinctions were disappearing.

Mind was disappearing; it was millions of miles away. It was difficult to catch hold of it, it was rushing farther and farther away, and there was no urge to keep it close. I was simply indifferent about it all. It was okay. There was no urge to remain continuous with the past.

By the evening it became so difficult to bear it—it was hurting, it was painful. It was like when a woman goes into labor when a child is to be born, and the woman suffers tremendous pain—the birth pangs.

I used to go to sleep on those days about twelve or one in the night, but that day it was impossible to remain awake. My eyes were closing, it was difficult to keep them open. Something was very imminent, something was going to happen. It was difficult to say what it was—maybe it is going to be my death—but there was no fear. I was ready for it. Those seven days had been so beautiful that I was ready to die, nothing more was needed. They had been so tremendously blissful, I was so contented, that if death was coming, it was welcome.

But something was going to happen—something like death, something very drastic, something which will be either a death or a new birth, a crucifixion or a resurrection—but something of tremendous import was just around the corner. And it was impossible to keep my eyes open. . . .

I went to sleep near about eight. It was not like sleep. Now I can understand what Patanjali[13] means when he says that sleep and *samadhi* are similar. Only with one difference—that in *sama-*

dhi you are fully awake and asleep also. Asleep and awake together, the whole body relaxed, every cell of the body totally
relaxed, all functioning relaxed, and yet a light of awareness
burns within you . . . clear, smokeless. You remain alert and yet
relaxed, loose but fully awake. The body is in the deepest sleep
possible and your consciousness is at its peak. The peak of consciousness and the valley of the body meet.

I went to sleep. It was a very strange sleep. The body was
asleep, I was awake. It was so strange—as if one was torn apart
into two directions, two dimensions; as if the polarity has become
completely focused, as if I was both the polarities together: the
positive and negative were meeting, sleep and awareness were
meeting, death and life were meeting. That is the moment when
you can say "the creator and the creation meet."

It was weird. For the first time it shocks you to the very roots,
it shakes your foundations. You can never be the same after that
experience; it brings a new vision to your life, a new quality.

Near about twelve my eyes suddenly opened—I had not
opened them. The sleep was broken by something else. I felt a
great presence around me in the room. It was a very small room.
I felt a throbbing life all around me, a great vibration—almost like
a hurricane, a great storm of light, joy, ecstasy. I was drowning in
it.

It was so tremendously real that everything became unreal.
The walls of the room became unreal, the house became unreal,
my own body became unreal . . .

That night another reality opened its door, another dimension
became available. Suddenly it was there, the other reality, the
separate reality, the really Real, or whatsoever you want to call
it—call it God, call it Truth, call it Dhamma, call it Tao, or whatsoever you will. It was nameless. But it was there—so opaque, so
transparent, and yet so solid one could have touched it. It was
almost suffocating me in that room. It was too much and I was
not yet capable of absorbing it.

A deep urge arose in me to rush out of the room, to go under
the sky—it was suffocating me. It was too much! It will kill me! If
I had remained a few moments more, it would have suffocated
me—it looked like that.

I rushed out of the room, came out in the street. A great urge was there just to be under the sky with the stars, with the trees, with the earth . . . to be with nature. And immediately as I came out, the feeling of being suffocated disappeared. It was too small a place for such a big phenomenon. Even the sky is a small place for that big phenomenon. . . . It is bigger than the sky. Even the sky is not the limit for it. But then I felt more at ease.

I was walking towards the nearest garden. It was a totally new walk, as if gravitation [gravity] had disappeared. I was walking, or I was running, or I was simply flying; it was difficult to decide. There was no gravitation, I was feeling weightless—as if some energy was taking me. I was in the hands of some other energy.

For the first time I was not alone, for the first time I was no more an individual, for the first time the drop had come and fallen into the ocean. Now the whole ocean was mine, I was the ocean. There was no limitation. A tremendous power arose as if I could do anything whatsoever. I was not there, only the power was there.

I reached the garden where I used to go every day. The garden was closed for the night. It was too late, it was almost one o'clock in the night. The gardeners were fast asleep. I had to enter the garden like a thief, I had to climb the gate. But something was pulling me towards the garden. It was not within my capacity to prevent myself. I was just floating.

That's what I mean when I say again and again, "Float with the river, don't push the river." I was relaxed, I was in a let-go. I was not there. IT was there, call it God—God was there.

The moment I entered the garden everything became luminous, it was all over the place—the benediction, the blessedness. I could see the trees for the first time—their green, their life, their very sap running. The whole garden was asleep, the trees were asleep. But I could see the whole garden alive, even the small grass leaves were so beautiful.

I looked around. One tree was tremendously luminous—the maulshree tree. It attracted me, it pulled me toward itself. I had not chosen it, God himself had chosen it. I went to the tree, I sat under the tree. As I sat there things started settling. The whole universe became a benediction.

It is difficult to say how long I was in that state. When I went back home it was four o'clock in the morning,[14] so I must have been there by clock time at least three hours—but it was infinity. It had nothing to do with clock time. It was timeless.

Those three hours became the whole eternity, endless eternity. There was no time, there was no passage of time; it was the virgin reality—uncorrupted, untouchable, unmeasurable.

And that day something happened that has continued—not as a continuity—but it has still continued as an undercurrent. Not as a permanency—each moment it has been happening again and again. It has been a miracle each moment.[15]

In a way, the story of Rajneesh ends right here. "There is no story after that explosion," says Bhagwan, "there are no events after it. All events are before the explosion. After the explosion there is only void."[16] His search came to an end and, in a way, the prediction of the astrologer finally came true. The man named Rajneesh Chandra Mohan died at twenty-one and yet the resurrection happened, the miracle happened. He was reborn, but not in the physical body; he attained something, but not of this world—he simply arrived home.

It needs to be mentioned here briefly that enlightenment is not a concept that can be explained in logical terms; rather it is an experience that transcends logic and verbal explanations. Similarly, enlightenment is not a thing that enables one to walk six feet off the ground or walk on water. I don't know what happened to Buddha when he became enlightened, but the phenomenon is intriguing and we venerate it.

In Bhagwan's case the event was, in a way, a miracle, and yet there was nothing miraculous about it. The bud had flowered; the hidden had become manifest. The flowering is a miracle and not a miracle; it is a miracle in the sense that the seed has been transformed into something unbelievable, and not a miracle because it is the culmination of a natural evolutionary process.

Bhagwan has repeatedly stressed that enlightenment is already present, it is already an integral part of our being—

it is not a thing to be achieved somewhere in the future. As Bhagwan points out, enlightenment is already available to us; one simply has to "relax into it." He explains:

An enlightened person is not somebody who has reached to the pinnacle, who has reached to the topmost rung of the ladder. You are *all* ladder climbers . . . you need a ladder. . . . Enlightenment is not the last rung of a ladder. Enlightenment is getting down from the ladder, getting down forever and never asking for any ladder again, becoming natural.[17]

Bhagwan warns us to beware of certain explanations about enlightenment since they can easily confuse seekers. Using Sri Aurobindo's description of "supra-consciousness" as an example, Bhagwan comments:

Enlightenment is a natural state. It is not some supra-conscious state, supra-mental. Avoid Sri Aurobindo and his terminology; that is all mind games. It [enlightenment] is not something very special; it is very ordinary. It is so ordinary that there is nothing to brag about in it.[18]

The story that follows Bhagwan's enlightenment is a new story, in the sense that it is not continuous with his past. From here on, he does not *do* anything because the ego—the sense of the *doer* and the *doing*—has ceased to exist. "That night I became empty and became full," says Bhagwan.

I became non-existential and became existence. That night I died and was reborn. But the one that was reborn has nothing to do with that which died, it is a discontinuous thing. . . . The one who died, died totally; nothing of him has remained . . . not even a shadow. It died totally, utterly. . . . That day of March twenty-first, the person who had lived for many, many lives, for millennia, simply died. Another being, absolutely new, not connected at all with the old, started to exist.[19]

The experience of that "death" was a religious one in its purest and most original sense. Bhagwan continues:

Religion just gives you a total death. Maybe that's why the whole day previous to that happening I was feeling some urgency like death, as if I was going to die—and I really died. I have known many other deaths, but they were nothing compared to it; they were partial deaths. Sometimes the body died, sometimes a part of the mind died, sometimes a part of the ego died, but as far as the person was concerned, it remained. Renovated many times, decorated many times, changed a little bit here and there, but it remained; the continuity remained.

That night the death was total. It was a date with death and God simultaneously.[20]

The event did not change either Bhagwan's routine or his lifestyle, however. He continued to attend classes at college whenever he felt like doing so, but remained busy mostly reading and writing. The reading he did then and later was, however, for a different purpose. Before enlightenment, his reading was part of his own search, while after that happening, reading became part of his work to help those who were still searching. Reading made it possible for Bhagwan to be familiar with current thinking, research, and terminology, and it has enabled him to communicate his thoughts and share his experiences in the most up-to-date manner, in the context of present-day living.

Rajneesh wrote for various newspapers and magazines in Hindi. His language and style were essentially poetic, and the thoughts were deep and profound. He was also in demand to give talks and to participate in debates in Jabalpur and other cities. His talks were original, fiery, and authentic.

Rajneesh completed his B.A. in philosophy in 1955, and began working toward his M.A. at the well-known Saugar University. At Saugar he lived in a student dormitory for two years. Rajneesh got his master's degree in philosophy (first division) in 1957 and was recognized as an outstanding student of the university. He enjoyed those two years tremendously, because he could immerse himself completely in the vast collection of the university library, and at the same time, enjoy a pleasant, natural setting surrounded by beautiful hills. Rather than attending classes, Rajneesh spent most of his time reading in the library and roaming at night under the starry sky, enjoying the raindrops or walk-ing in the hills. Even on holidays when the library was closed, he could be found reading on the library lawn or wandering with nature as his only company.

His life for these two years at Saugar remained as inter-esting as ever and reflected the same essential qualities of rebelliousness and experimentation that he had shown all along. It did not matter to him whether or not what he did conformed with the dictates of family, society, school, or religion.

Bhagwan explains that one does not *become* integrated, one is already integrated deep inside, though on the pe-riphery there is much turmoil; hence, one only needs to move inward. And the deeper one goes inside, the more one finds that he or she is already integrated. How to dis-cover it? For this he suggests: "Only do that which you enjoy doing. If you do not enjoy, don't do it." He relates his own experiment:

I used to do it in my university days, and people thought that I was crazy: suddenly I would stop, and . . . remain in that spot for half an hour, an hour, unless I started enjoying walking again. My professors were so afraid that, when there were examinations, they would put me in a car and take me to the university hall. They would leave me at the door and wait there: had I reached my desk or not? If I was taking my bath and suddenly I realized that I was not enjoying it, I would stop. What is the point then? If I was eating and I recognized suddenly that I was not enjoying [it], then I would stop.[21]

Similarly, once during his school days in Gadarwara, he got up in the middle of his first mathematics class in high school and told his teacher he would not come back because he did not enjoy the class. "And by and by," points out Bhagwan, "it became a key. I suddenly recognized that whenever you are enjoying something, you are centered. Enjoyment is just the sound of being centered. Whenever you are not enjoying something, you are off center."[22]

One can gain a perspective on Bhagwan's life by understanding his experiment with the three *gunas*—the three basic qualities that make up the human personality. An individual of *tamas guna* shows inactivity, inertia, indolence; one of *rajas guna* exhibits intense activity or passion; and a person of *sattva guna* has the quality of serenity, calmness, and wisdom. Lord Krishna has elaborated upon these gunas in the *Bhagavad Gita*.[23]

Generally, all three gunas are present in all individuals in different proportions. The mixture of these three gunas in each person contributes to the formation of each individual's personality. No matter how predominant one quality may be in a person, the other two are also there, even if dormant.

Commenting upon the past Buddhas—Jesus, Mohammed, Lao Tzu, Ramana Maharshi, and Krishna—Bhagwan has this to say:

Rajas was the predominant medium of expression for Jesus and Mohammed. *Tamas* was the predominant quality of Lao Tzu and Ramana Maharshi. But Krishna made use of all the three qualities simultaneously as his medium of expression. Just as the equilateral triangle has three lines of equal length, in the personality of Krishna all three gunas are present and united in equal measure.[24]

Because of this, Krishna is not consistent and, therefore, Krishna's life and actions have been very much misunderstood. In contrast, Buddha, Lao Tzu, Mohammed, and Jesus are quite consistent, because they exhibit one predominant quality. Bhagwan has exhibited all three gunas as Krishna did, but with one difference: Bhagwan has used them sequentially rather than simultaneously. "In my opinion this is the most scientific way of doing it, and that is why I have chosen this way," says Bhagwan.[25]

Reflecting further upon the similarities between Krishna's personality and his own, Bhagwan explains:

In me also there will be inconsistency, but not so much as in Krishna. There is another possibility which I have utilized in my own experiments. All three gunas are present in every individual, and a personality can be complete and total only when all three are utilized. None of the gunas need be suppressed. Neither is Krishna in favor of suppression, nor am I in favor of suppression. Whatsoever there is in an individual must be utilized creatively.[26]

Throughout the early period of his life Rajneesh was often regarded as lazy and of no help to the family. This, however, was due to the fact that he often experimented with the quality of *tamas* (inactivity, indolence).

The first years of my life were spent like Lao Tzu, in experiencing the mysteries of the tamas guna. My attachment to Lao Tzu is, therefore, fundamental. I was inactive in everything; inactivity was the achievement sought by me. As far as possible, nothing was done—only as much as was unavoidable or compulsory. I did not do so much as move a hand or a foot without a reason.[27]

An illustration:

In my house, the situation was such that my mother sitting before me would say, "Nobody else can be found and I want to send someone to fetch vegetables from the market." I would hear this as I sat idly in front of her. I knew that even if the house was on fire, she would say to me, "No one else can be found and our house is on fire, who will extinguish it?" But silently, the only thing I did was to watch my inactivity as a witness, in full awareness.[28]

During this period, the quality of inactivity became significant for Bhagwan in his overall experimentation with the three gunas.

In my own experiments I chose to express one guna at a time—only one in a single time period. First I chose tamas . . . because this principle is in the basic foundation of everyone. When a child is growing in the mother's womb for nine months, it is living in this guna. The child does not do anything on its own. It is in a condition of total inactivity.[29]

Bhagwan finds this guna not only the predominant one, but he also shows how the state of inactivity in the womb is significant in a spiritual sense.

The child has known supreme silence in the womb. This memory is hidden deep down in the unconscious. That nine-month experience in the mother's womb was very blissful, because then there was nothing to be done. . . . There was only existence for you—just being. This state is very similar to the state we call liberation.[30]

Bhagwan thus teaches that the search for a silent and blissful state is not accidental—rather it is related to our deep unconscious; it is a search for the blissful state of the womb. But there is one crucial difference between life in the womb and any attempt to re-experience it. The state in the womb is part of the biological process of growth and the child is not conscious of the state, but in the remembrance or revival of that state at the peak of spiritual experience, the individual is fully conscious. Bhagwan uses a metaphor to describe the function of tamas guna:

Inactivity is the foundation, and blissful silence is the crest. This house which we call life is built on the foundation of inactivity. The middle structure is the active part and the dome of that temple is ultimate bliss. In my opinion, this is the edifice of life. That is why I . . . practiced inactivity in the first part of my life.[31]

In Bhagwan's experiments with each of the three gunas, one constant factor was his watchfulness, his awareness, his remaining a witness to each state, his being an unidentified observer. He describes the nature of this awareness by relating the following story:

In the last year of my university education, there was one professor of philosophy. Like most professors of philosophy, he was obstinate and eccentric. He was obstinate in his determination not to see any woman. Unfortunately there were only two students in his class: . . . myself and . . . a young girl. Therefore, this professor had to teach us while keeping his eyes closed.

This was a very lucky thing for me, because while he would give a lecture I would sleep in class. Because there was a young girl in the class he could not open his eyes. However, the professor was very pleased with me, because he thought that I also believed in the principle of not looking at women, and that in the whole university there was at least one other person who did not see women. Therefore, many times when he met me alone he told me that I was the only person who could understand him.

But one day this image of me was erased. The professor had one other habit. He did not believe in a one-hour period for his lectures. Therefore, he was always given the last period by the university. He would say, "It is in my hands when to begin a lecture, but it is not in my hands to end it." Therefore, his lecture might end in sixty minutes or eighty minutes or even ninety minutes; it made no difference to him. . . .

There was an understanding between the young girl and myself that she would wake me up when the period was near to end. One day, however, she had been called by someone for some urgent work during the middle of the period, and she went away. I kept on sleeping and the professor went on lecturing. When the period was over and he opened his eyes, he found me sleeping. He woke me up and asked why I was sleeping. I said to him, "Now that you have found me sleeping, I would like to tell you that I have been sleeping daily, that I have no quarrel with young women and that it is very pleasurable to sleep while you are lecturing.[32]

During these years sleeping had become a sort of meditation for Rajneesh. He came to know during his experiments with sleep what Krishna had conveyed to Arjuna:

"Even though the rest of the world remains asleep at night, the sage is always awake."[33] Rajneesh experienced wakefulness, the witnessing state, in his sleep. This is different from the sleep in which one remains unconscious. Rajneesh found out that if one persisted in sleeping more than the body requirement then "someone inside you remains aware and becomes a witness of all that is happening around you . . . then within you a sort of wakeful sound begins to become audible."[34]

Bhagwan describes his life at Saugar University during this inactive phase:

I made it my first principle to refrain from doing anything. For the two years that I was in the university hostel, I never cleaned or swept my room. I kept my cot right at the entrance of my room so that from the door I could jump straight into my cot and from the cot I could jump straight out of the room. Why should the whole room be unnecessarily traversed, I felt. Neither did I want to enter into the room, nor was there any question of cleaning it. There was, however, a sort of joy in this.

Things were left in the same way that they had been arranged prior to my living there, no change was made. No more was ever done than the minimum that was necessary. Because changing things around required that something be done, things were kept as they were. But due to this, some unique experiences began to dawn, as every guna has its own unique experience. No matter how much rubbish became collected in my room, it did not disturb me at all. I had learned to live with that condition just as I would live in a place which is meticulously cleaned.

In the university where I was studying, new buildings were as yet not constructed. It was a newly established university, and military barracks were used as a hostel. Because the barracks were in a deep forest it was frequently common for snakes to appear. I used to watch those snakes while sleeping on my cot. The snakes came, rested in the room and went away. Neither did they disturb me at any time, not did I disturb them.[35]

In his experiments with sleep and inactivity, Rajneesh also experienced the state of no-mind, or the experience of having no thoughts—the state of being a pure consciousness.

In those days I used to go on lying upon the cot, vacantly watching the ceiling above. I came to know after a long time that Meher Baba had meditated in this manner only. I did this without any effort, because while lying down on a cot what else is there to do? If the sleep was over, I would just go on looking at the ceiling without even blinking the eyes. Why even blink the eyes? It is also a type of doing. It is also a part of activity. I just went on lying there. There was nothing to be done. If you remain lying down like that, just looking at the ceiling for an hour or two, you will find that your mind becomes clear like a cloudless sky—just thoughtless. If someone can make inactivity his achievement in life, he can experience thoughtlessness very naturally and easily.[36]

This state of non-doing and no-mind opened up the doors of divine glory to him.

In those days I neither believed in God nor in the soul. The only reason for not believing was that by believing something would have to be done. For inactivity, atheism is very helpful, because if God is, then some work will have to be done for him. But without any belief on my part in God and soul, by my simply lying down silently, the effulgent splendor of both God and soul began to be visualized. I did not give up inactivity until inactivity left me. Until then, I had decided to continue on like that—just doing nothing.[37]

All this time, while Rajneesh was at school in Jabalpur, his paternal grandmother was very eager for him to get married. She kept pushing the family, especially Rajneesh's father, Dadda, to arrange his marriage. Dadda's friends also kept urging Rajneesh's marriage, but Dadda was hesitant to even propose the idea to his son. He knew very well that suggesting to Rajneesh that he marry would mean taking a big chance, for if Rajneesh said no, then that would be the end of the whole matter.

Nevertheless, when Bhagwan came home after graduating from the university, Dadda, indirectly through Rajneesh's friends, tried to find out if he would be interested in marrying. Rajneesh felt that Dadda himself should ask this question directly. Dadda was hesitant; finally, he asked Bhagwan's mother to go and talk to him. As Bhagwan tells the story:

. . . One night she came to my bed, sat there, and asked me what I thought about marriage. So I said, "I have not married yet, so I have no experience. You know well, you have the experience, so you tell me. Take fifteen days: think over it, contemplate, and if you feel you have achieved something through it, then just order me. I will follow the order. Don't ask about my opinion. I have none, because I have no experience. You are experienced. If you were again given a chance, would you get married?"

She said, "You are trying to confuse me."

I said, "You take your time, at your own ease. I will wait for two weeks, then you order me. I will just follow, because I don't know."

So for two weeks she was worried. She could not sleep because she knew if she said to marry, I would follow. Then she would be responsible, not I. So after two weeks she said, "I am not going to say anything, because if I look to my own experience, then I would not like you to move into that life. But I cannot say anything now."

So this is how I remained unmarried. Sincerely, authentically, I was not ready to marry, I was not intending [to] at all.[38]

As seen earlier, Bhagwan remained mainly in the state of tamas, inactivity, throughout his school and college years. But after obtaining his master's degree, he entered into the state of rajas guna and became very active. He remained in the fiery rajas throughout the following years until he began to manifest the cool sattva guna and finally settled down in Poona in 1974.

5. Neo-Sannyas:
The Lotus in a Swamp

AFTER HE graduated from the university, Rajneesh
looked for a teaching job. The rebelliousness that he had
shown all along came through once again when he was
interviewed for a job. He narrates the incident as follows:

When I came out of the university, I applied for a government
job. The education minister called me for an interview and asked
me for some character certificates [references].

I said, "I am here; you look at me. I can sit here, you can
watch me. I can live with you for a few days if you like. But don't
ask about certificates. Who can give me a character certificate?"

He couldn't understand. He said, "You can bring one from
your vice-chancellor, or at least from the head of your department." I said, "If my vice-chancellor asks for a character certificate . . . I am not going to give it to him. So how can I ask for a
character certificate from him? I cannot give one to him. So that
is impossible. I can ask for a character certificate only from a man
whom I can see is a man of character. But that will be absurd.
That means that first I give him a character certificate—only then
his character certificate becomes meaningful."

But he could not follow me. He said, "Then it will be difficult,
because at least two character certificates are needed."

So I wrote a character reference in the name of my vice-chancellor. And I went to the vice-chancellor later on and said . . . this
is the certificate I have given to myself. You have to sign it."

He said, "But this is absurd. How can you give a character
certificate . . . [for] yourself?"

I told him, "If I cannot give . . . [one for] myself, then who can give one to me? I know myself more than anybody else knows me. You don't know me at all. If you can give a character certificate to me, then why can't I? This is the certificate. You have to sign it."

He looked at the certificate and laughed, because I had written on the certificate that man is a freedom, and character is always of the past, and the future remains open. I may have been a good man up to now. Next moment? Nobody knows! I may have been a saint up to now, but the next moment I can become a sinner. In fact, each moment I have to give a new lease to my character, again and again and again I have to hold it.[1]

By this explanation, Bhagwan impressed those who were involved in the process of his hiring, and he was appointed to a teaching position at Sanskrit Mahavidyalaya, Raipur (Raipur Sanskrit College), in 1957. By 1960 he was a professor of philosophy at the University of Jabalpur.

Throughout his teaching career, Bhagwan was known as a brilliant and wonderful teacher. He inspired interest and a spirit of investigation in his students and encouraged them to search for answers on their own. He was so popular that students often left other classes to sit in on his.

Bhagwan's rebelliousness continued to show right from the day he started his job at Raipur Sanskrit College. The following incident narrated by Bhagwan attests to this:

I was a professor in a Sanskrit university. The first day I reached the university I was not yet allotted quarter[s] so I had to stay in the hostel for a few days. Because it was a Sanskrit university . . . and nobody wants to learn Sanskrit nowadays—it is a dead language, it serves no purpose, it will not help you earn your bread and butter—almost ninety percent of the students were on government scholarships. They were there only because of the scholarships. They had no desire to learn Sanskrit, they were not interested in it, but they were poor students and they could not get scholarships anywhere else. So it was better than nothing. . . . And because they were almost all scholarship holders, they were forced to pray every morning at four o'clock. . . .

When I reached the university it was wintertime, and by four o'clock they were shivering and they were taking cold baths. No hot water was provided—Sanskrit scholars are not supposed to have such luxuries as hot water; they are supposed to live like the ancient rishis[2] and their disciples. And they used to get up early, at four o'clock, brahma muhurta; this is one of the most divine moments according to the Hindu mythology. . . .

They did not know that I was a professor that first day. I loved to have a cold bath in the morning, so I went to the well to take a bath. And the students were so angry: they were using all kinds of four-letter words . . . not only about the vice-chancellor but about God also. . . .

I reported to the vice-chancellor: "This is not right. You are not teaching them prayer. And then after the cold bath they have to stand in a line and pray for hours in Sanskrit. Now, how can they be prayerful? They are angry with God. If they come across God they will kill him! And they are praying, so what kind of prayer can it be?"

But the vice-chancellor was an old Sanskrit scholar. He said, "No, that's not right. They are doing it on their own; we are not forcing anybody."

I said, "I know that they are doing it on their own, because if they don't do it their scholarships disappear. You are not forcing them in a direct, but an indirect way. And if you want to argue with me, then give me only one day and I will put up a notice saying that whoever wants to have a cold bath at four o'clock and pray can get up, and whoever does not want to need not worry about the scholarship; it will be up to him."

Now the vice-chancellor was caught; he had to agree. . . . And I went to the vice-chancellor at four o'clock—he himself was asleep. I dragged him out of bed. I said, "Come on! What kind of vice-chancellor are you? Your students are praying, taking cold baths, and you are asleep!"

He was very angry at me. I said, "The same is happening to them. Come on!"

And there was not a single student there! The well was empty, the prayer hall was empty. I told him, "Now take a cold bath with me, and we will both pray!"

He said, "I cannot take a cold bath. I am an old man!"

I said, "Okay, then I will take the cold bath. You sit here and watch, and then we will go and pray."

He said, "But I am feeling tired and I want to go to sleep!"

"Then," I said, "I am the only person who will be praying—and I don't know Sanskrit at all! And God understands only Sanskrit! I was wrongly appointed to this university by the mistake of the Ministry of Education. They thought, looking at me, that I must know Sanskrit. I don't know Sanskrit at all. I am not interested in anything dead."

So he went to his room and I went to my room, and everybody slept. And that morning the students came to me and they were so happy, they were so thankful.

And I said to the vice-chancellor, "This is far more beautiful, this is far more prayerful—their coming to me and thanking me." I said to him, "Stop all this nonsense!"

But rather than stopping the nonsense he made the government transfer me to another university, saying, "This man is dangerous! He will destroy my students' morality, character, religion."[3]

After a year Bhagwan was assigned to the faculty at Jabalpur University. During this period, he spent much time exercising and building up his body. Keeping himself in excellent physical health was in line with things, for over the next ten years the growing rajas energy kept him constantly on the move. He traveled all over the country with great passion and intensity. In building up his body, Bhagwan was perhaps aware of what a toll the following years would take.

The hectic traveling that followed after 1960 shows the rajas (activity) phase of his life. This activity, according to Bhagwan, is possible when one has thoroughly lived out or transcended inactivity and develops automatically—it flows naturally from within. Bhagwan explains that this activity is totally different from the anxiety-ridden and tense kind that a politician might experience. Unlike a politician's activity, this activity is motivated not by desire but by compassion.

Bhagwan fully lived through this activity phase before he settled down in Bombay in 1970. Bhagwan describes this phase of his life as follows:

When this second phase—that of rajas—began, I kept on running throughout the country. As much as I traveled within those ten to fifteen years, no one would travel even in [the span of] two or three lives [births]. As much as I spoke during those ten to fifteen years would ordinarily require [someone else] ten to fifteen lives [births]. From morning until night I was on the move, traveling everywhere.[4]

Describing the purpose and nature of this phase, Bhagwan says:

With or without reason, I was creating controversies and making criticism—because the more the controversies, the quicker this transition through the second phase of activity. I therefore began to criticize Gandhiji [Mahatma Gandhi], I began to criticize socialism.

Neither did I have any relationship with these subjects, nor was there any attachment to politics. I had no interest whatever in these. But when the entire population of the country was absorbed in these tensions . . . there seemed, even if just for fun, a necessity to create controversies. Therefore, during this transition of my second phase of activity, I engineered a number of controversies and enjoyed them.

If those controversies had been created due to tension-filled actions motivated by desire, it would have brought me unhappiness. But as all this was just . . . to develop the rajas guna, just for its expression, there was fun and interest in it. These controversies were just like the acting of an actor.[5]

The hectic nature of his travels and the nature of his talks are described by Bhagwan as follows:

For three weeks out of a month I was sitting on trains. One morning I would be in Bombay, the next evening I would be in Calcutta, the next day in Amritsar, and the following day in Ludhiana or Delhi. The whole country was the field of my operations. Everywhere, therefore, wherever I went, controversies naturally grew in abundance. . . .[6]

While he was passing through the phase of inactivity, Bhagwan spoke very little. But Bhagwan says, "During the period of activity, I went myself to people just to speak, and my language was full of fire. . . . "

That fire was not mine. It came out of the rajas guna. That was only one method for burning out the fire of the rajas guna. It must burn in full ferocity so that it can turn to ashes quickly. The milder the fire, the longer it takes to burn out. It was, therefore, a process of total burning out for the purpose of a speedier reduction to ashes.[7]

An important development of this period occurred in 1964. In that year Bhagwan first introduced meditation to followers at a ten-day meditation camp held in the hills of Rajasthan (one of the states in western India), at a place called Muchala Mahavir. He taught several kinds of meditation that could be practiced in the early morning and during the day, as well as in the evening and before going to bed. Some of the meditation techniques such as Vipassana, Nadabrahma, and Whirling are well known to meditators of different traditions.

Bhagwan has explained what meditation is in innumerable ways and in great depth. He calls meditation essentially "a state of no-mind," which is a state of cessation of thoughts, a state of silence:

The mind is a constant traffic: thoughts are moving, desires are moving, memories are moving, ambitions are moving . . . when there is no traffic and thinking has ceased, no thoughts move, no desire stirs, you are utterly silent—that silence is meditation. In that silence truth is known, and never otherwise. Meditation is a state of no-mind.[8]

Contrary to popular notion, Bhagwan does not look upon meditation as a serious activity. Meditation, according to him, is an experience of nonactivity, joy, and playfulness:

Mind is very serious, and meditation is absolutely nonserious. When I say this you may be bewildered, because people go on talking about meditation very seriously. But meditation is not a serious thing. It is just like play . . . sincere, but nonserious. It is not something like work; it is more like play. Play is not an activity. Even when it is active, it is not an activity. Play is just pleasure. The activity is not going anywhere; it is not motivated. Rather, it is just pure, flowing energy.[9]

After the first meditation camp held in 1964, Bhagwan traveled far and wide conducting such camps all over the country. He usually chose places in a natural setting away from crowds and city noise. These meditation camps and his discourses became instantly popular and he began to stir the nation. He began to have a significant impact upon people from all walks of life, and more and more people fell in love with him.

Bhagwan's frequent travels, his style and originality, his sharp wit and rebellious nature often annoyed the university administration, however, because of his popularity and reputation, they could do nothing. His friends often insisted that he give up his job so that he could devote full time and energy to his work. Bhagwan would reply that this would happen when God wished it.

In 1966, he felt that the time had come for him to free himself from the university job. He was asked to resign amid the usual controversy in August, 1966, having just returned from a tour. For a number of years, Bhagwan had been wearing a *lungi* (a long piece of cloth wrapped below the waist) and *chadar* (a long piece of cloth wrapped around the body above the waist). Although college officials had previously expressed their dislike of this style of dress, the principal chose Bhagwan's return from his tour to press the issue. Since Bhagwan never objected to the kind of clothes the principal wore, he felt it was unjust for the principal to object to his style of dress. When pressed by the principal, Bhagwan immediately submitted his letter of resignation, which he always carried with him.

Free from his teaching work at Jabalpur University, Bhagwan now began unraveling his rajas energy by speaking out on such controversial issues as Mahatma Gandhi, sex, orthodox Hindu religion, and socialism. He openly and boldly criticized Mahatma Gandhi, his ideas, and his followers during the Gandhi Centenary Year, 1968–1969. Bhagwan's criticism of Gandhi is twofold: first, he finds Gandhi a man of ethics, not of religion. Bhagwan does not see Gandhi as a religious man, even though that is how Gandhi is popularly known in India, because Gandhi did not have any experience of meditation. Bhagwan points out, moreover, that Gandhi's whole concept of religious synthesis was not free from his bias toward Hinduism. In Bhagwan's words:

Gandhi knew nothing of meditation, but he tried hard to create a certain façade of synthesis. Basically, he was a Hindu and he remained a Hindu all his life, to the very end. He calls the Bhagavad Gita his mother, but he never calls the Koran his father—nor even an uncle. Although he says that the teaching is the same, the way he manages it is absolutely political—clever, cunning, but not authentic . . . . Whatever he finds in the Koran, in the Bible, in the Dhammapada, which is in agreement with the Gita, he immediately picks up and he says, "Look! All the religions teach the same thing!"

But there are many things which go against the Gita in the Bible, which go against the Gita in the Koran, in the Dhammapada. He does not take any notice of them, he ignores them . . . so his synthesis is bogus. In fact, he reads the Gita everywhere, wherever he can find the Gita echoes, he immediately says, "Look! They are saying the same thing!"

But what about the differences? What about the totally opposite standpoints?

Gandhi chooses only pieces and then makes a hodgepodge

which he calls the synthesis of all religions. It never happened. Neither the Moslems were convinced by him, nor the Hindus. . . . And he was murdered by a Hindu.[10]

Describing his own vision of religion and in that context explaining the nature of his work, Bhagwan said in March, 1971:

I am . . . not a synthesizer like Gandhiji. I do not call for any synthesizing of religions. I am saying that all religions, with their own distinct individualities, are acceptable to me. . . .[11]

The Koran and the Gita are not one, but a link can be made joining the two. So I would like to spread a network of sannyasins who are such that they would form the links. These sannyasins will do *namaj* in a mosque, say prayers in a church and do *kirtan* [Hindu devotional chanting] in a temple also. They will walk on the path of Mahavir, meditate as Buddha did and even experiment with the Sikh tradition; thus making connecting links —a living chain of human links. All will be struck by the one religious feeling that all religions, *though separate,* are one: not that all religions are one and inseparable, but that *though* they are separate, they are one in their inner harmonious march toward the goal. They are one in the sense that they lead you toward one superconsciousness.[12]

The overall perspective which I have before me is this: that I would like to help every person to move according to his capacity, his stage of evolution, his culture—according to what has already been assimilated in his blood. Then it will be much easier for him to achieve. Therefore, I have neither any religion of my own, nor any path of my own, because now one exclusive path or religion will not work for the future. . . .[13]

Bhagwan also finds Gandhi's view of society and his solutions to its problems primitive and nonscientific. He finds them regressive because they are rooted in tradition. Bhagwan points out that Gandhi was more in favor of the old means, one example of which was his propagating the spinning wheel, rather than more modern, advanced technological means. In Bhagwan's view, Gandhi was not in favor of the modernization of India which is critically needed.

In matters of sex and reproduction, Gandhi strongly advocated self-control and celibacy, which Bhagwan finds impractical. Bhagwan draws our attention to the dangers of population explosion and hence supports modern methods of birth control.

Gandhi's poverty-worshipping ideas are totally unacceptable to Bhagwan. Gandhi deified poverty by calling the poor *daridra narayan*.[14] Bhagwan says poverty has to be destroyed, not perpetuated. For this, he says, the sooner India comes out of her age-old superstitions and beliefs, which Gandhi himself followed, and steps into the twentieth century, the better.

For twenty years I have criticized Mahatma Gandhi and his philosophy. No Gandhian has answered. Many Gandhians have come to me and they say, "Whatever you say is right, but we cannot say it in public, because if we say that whatever you say about Mahatma Gandhi is right, we will lose. The public believes in Mahatma Gandhi." So utter nonsense has to be supported because Gandhi was antitechnological. Now this country will remain poor if this country remains antitechnological; this country will never be in a state of well-being. And there is no need for technology always to be anti-ecology, there is no need. Technology can be developed which can be in tune with ecology. Technology can be developed which can help people and will not destroy nature. But Gandhi is against technology.

He was against the railway, he was against the post office. He was against electricity, he was against machines of all kinds. They know this is stupid . . . and they go on paying homage to Mahatma Gandhi because they have to get the votes from the people. And the people worship the Mahatma, because the Mahatma fits with their ideas of how a mahatma should be.

Mahatma Gandhi fits with the Indian mob. The Indian mob worships him. The politician has to follow the mob. Remember always: in politics the leader follows the followers. He has to. He only pretends that he is leading; deep down he has to follow the followers. Once the followers leave him, he is nowhere. He cannot stand on his own, he has no ground of his own.

Gandhi worshipped poverty. Now if you worship poverty, you will remain poor. Poverty has to be hated. I hate poverty! I cannot say "Worship it." That would be a crime. And I don't see any religious quality in just being poor. But Gandhi talked much about poverty and its beauty; it helps the poor man's ego; it buttresses his ego. He feels good. It is a consolation that he is religious, simple; that he is poor. He may not have riches, but he has some spiritual richness. Poverty in itself is not a spiritual richness; no, not at all. Poverty is ugly and poverty has to be destroyed. And to destroy poverty, technology has to be brought in.

Mahatma Gandhi was against birth control. Now if you are against birth control . . . [India] will become every day poorer and poorer. Then there is no possibility.[15]

Bhagwan's talks on Gandhi created a great storm all over India, but especially in Gandhi's home state of Gujarat. One example of the anger and protest generated can be seen in the fact that many who claimed to be Bhagwan's friends left him. Also, an earlier promise of six hundred acres of land by the Gujarat government was revoked; the land would have provided Bhagwan with an ideal location to conduct meditation sessions.

Bhagwan added more fuel to the fire on August 28, 1968. He was invited by a group of friends to give a series of lectures on "love." The lecture was held at one of the prominent cultural and educational centers in Bombay, Bharatiya Vidya Bhavan. The lecture was in Hindi and what Bhagwan said in this lecture was totally unexpected. The main theme of his lecture was:

What I want to say is this: sex is divine. The primal energy of sex has the reflection of God in it. It is obvious: it is the energy that creates new life. And that is the greatest, most mysterious force of all.

End this enmity with sex. If you crave a shower of love in your life, renounce this conflict with sex. Accept sex with joy. Acknowledge its sacredness. Receive it gratefully and embrace it more and more deeply. You will be surprised that sex can reveal such sacredness; it will reveal its sacredness to the degree of your acceptance. And as sinful and irreverent as your approach is, that is how ugly and sinful the sex that confronts you will be. . . .

If you want to know the elemental truth about love, the first requisite is to accept the sacredness of sex, to accept the divinity of sex in the same way you accept God's existence—with an open heart. And the more fully you accept sex with an open heart and mind, the freer you will be of it. But the more you suppress it, the more you will become bound to it. . . .[16]

The lecture series was cancelled and Bhagwan returned to Jabalpur. But despite the fact that in this lecture Bhagwan jolted orthodox Indian beliefs, taboos, and attitudes about sex, he nevertheless simultaneously created enough interest in some people who listened to him that he was reinvited to continue the lectures. Exactly a month later, Bhagwan returned to Bombay and lectured on the same subject (September 28 through October 2) in an open public meeting before fifteen thousand people at Gowalia Tank Maidan.

In these lectures Bhagwan dealt with many aspects of sex and love, although his emphasis remained on transcending or purifying the sex energy into experiencing the divine. He strongly rejects the idea of celibacy, for he feels that celibacy is usually sexual suppression and not a healthy, natural tranformation of sex. He teaches that sex is a natural phenomenon and that people should experience it lovingly and meditatively so that it can become the *first step* on the way to superconsciousness. Bhagwan does not teach "free sex" or sexual indulgence, as is widely misunderstood. On the contrary, he has declared in unequivocal terms that sex, understood correctly, does not allow self-indulgence.

When these speeches were published, they brought Bhagwan nothing but anger and abuse from the public and the Indian press. But no one could give a sensible, intelligent, and unbiased response to the issues and aspects of sex discussed by Bhagwan. These discourses were translated into English in the book *From Sex to Superconsciousness,* published in 1979.

In March, 1969, Bhagwan was invited to speak at the Second World Hindu Religion Conference at Patna, the capital of the eastern state of Bihar. The conference was presided over by the highest religious priest of the Hindus, the Shankaracharya of Puri. This man objected to Bhagwan's presence on the same podium, and became angry and agitated about it. The organizers apologized and the Shankaracharya, somewhat mollified, allowed Bhagwan to have forty-five minutes. Bhagwan began lashing out at organized religions, the priests, and the hypocrisy of religion. He said:

Any religion which considers life meaningless and full of misery and teaches the hatred of life is not a true religion. Religion is an art that shows how to enjoy life. Liberation is not in running away from life, but rather in enjoying fully the life and the world. . . . But these shops [institutionalized religions] which are being run in the name of religion do not want . . . a person . . . [to] become truly religious. Because then these shops will have to be shut down, and there will no longer be any need for a priest or a world teacher. . . .[17]

Bhagwan had hardly spoken for ten minutes when Shankaracharya and his colleagues demanded that the organizers stop Bhagwan's lecture. Bhagwan asked the audience whether he should stop or continue. The audience shouted back that he should continue. At the conclusion of his lecture, the audience gave him very warm and loud applause, which made the Shankaracharya even more upset. Bhagwan said:

For me it was play, but for him it was a question of his very profession. He was so enraged that he had to be rescued from nearly falling down from the pulpit. His whole body was shaking.[18]

After independence from British rule, the leaders of the Congress Party, including Nehru, became committed to the ideas of socialism. India's economic plans and programs were built on the principles of socialism. Bhagwan expressed his total disagreement with the socialist ideals. He considers it disastrous for any country to talk about socialism without first building a capitalist economy. He does not regard capitalism and socialism as opposite systems. In July, 1969, Bhagwan spoke in Jabalpur on "India and Socialism." In his view:

Socialism is the ultimate result of capitalism. It is a very natural process. There is no need to go through any revolution. In fact, capitalism itself is a revolution that brings about socialism. Capitalism has shown, for the first time in the world, how to create wealth. I believe that in India socialism is inevitable, but fifty, sixty, or seventy years hence. India should apply all its best efforts to first creating wealth. The poverty in this country is so chronic, it has lasted for so long, that unless this country develops a capitalist system for the next fifty or one hundred years, this country will remain poor forever. Capitalism would make it possible to distribute wealth. At present, in the name of socialism, what we have for distribution is only poverty.[19]

Bhagwan's criticism of socialism and his support for capitalism brought an instant reaction: he was branded an antinational and called "a CIA agent."

Thus, with his talks, debates, and discussions, Bhagwan touched upon the very issues that were at the core of India's problems and maladies. Even at the risk of his life, Bhagwan made bold and frank statements for one reason: he strongly felt that India could no longer afford to push its dirt under the carpet. Someone had to take the lead in exposing the evils and stupidity that engulfed the country. Bhagwan gave that leadership and with his insight provided a glimpse of the vision he was going to unfold in the next ten years.

On his visits to Bombay, Bhagwan held meditation sessions at Palm Beach High School, Bombay, in the mornings. During his visit of April 13–16, 1970, Bhagwan surprised everyone who had come prepared for his regular "relax" meditation. He introduced for the first time his own technique of meditation, Dynamic Meditation. Having conducted "relax" meditation for many years, Bhagwan had found that the meditation did not really suit the needs of modern people. He explains:

I was working for ten years continuously with Lao Tzuan methods, so I was continuously teaching direct relaxation. It was simple for me so I thought it would be simple for everyone. Then, by and by, I became aware that it is impossible. . . . I would say "relax" to those I was teaching. They would appear to understand the meaning of the word but they could not relax. Then I had to devise new methods for meditation which create tension first—more tension. They create such tension that you become just mad. And then I say "relax."[20]

So the day he introduced Dynamic Meditation, everyone was taken aback and fascinated at the same time. The Indian press expressed its shock at watching the participants scream, shout, take off their clothes—the whole scene appeared weird and was certainly very intense. On the fourth day, the last day, Bhagwan said, "I have given you a very valuable technique. Do it regularly!"

The technique of Dynamic Meditation consists of elements from the Yoga, Sufi, and Tibetan traditions as well as findings of contemporary psychology. Bhagwan has pulled them together into one unique prescription suitable to meet the needs of individuals in contemporary society.[21] Beside Dynamic Meditation, other techniques taught by Bhagwan are simple and yet powerful, intense and yet playful. Music and movement are the two main components of these meditations, and the principle of the transformation of energy, by arousing activity and silently witnessing it, is at the core.

Meditation, according to Bhagwan, is an inward passive receptivity to all that is in the moment. Meditation is an impartial witnessing to whatever is happening. There are many processes that slow down body functions, bring relaxation, or reduce physical and mental stress, but they are not necessarily meditative processes. Certain drugs, music, and mantras (such as those used by the Transcendental Meditation movement) create a very definite slowing down—drugs by changing the body chemistry, the mantras of Transcendental Meditation by creating monotonous repetition. While some of these means may be healthy for the body in that they produce a deeper sleep, lower blood pressure, and so on, these body states do not necessarily have anything to do with spirituality, that is, with witnessing one's body, thoughts, and emotions as if they did not belong to you.

The body is the beginning; in meditation, one must start with the body, but there is a long way to go after that. One must go through emotions and thoughts as well. That is why Bhagwan's meditation techniques *start* with the body, to release the many physical suppressions and blocks that prevent an "opening" a detached witnessing. Once these blocks are released, the more subtle part of the technique takes effect. Once empty of all physical blocks, one is just an empty passage for energy to move in and be alchemically transmuted. If, for example, sex is a block, or if anger is a block, then the energy cannot go beyond sex or anger. If, on the other hand, sex and anger are released, then one can move to the heart and the mind—then there is nothing to impede the flow of energy.

Thus, the release, the physical and emotional catharsis, has an important place in the techniques devised by Bhagwan. In being "civilized," modern humans carry repressed feelings and emotions. This repression keeps them tense and often leads toward neurosis. Hence, unless this repression is released, the experience of being in meditation can never take place. Bhagwan explains, therefore, that

cathartic methods are modern inventions. In Buddha's time they were not needed, because people were not so repressed. People were natural, people lived primitive lives—uncivilized, spontaneous, lives. I am introducing cathartic methods, so that first what civilization has done to you can be undone, so that you become primitive again. From that primitiveness, from primal innocence, insight becomes easily available.[22]

Throughout his travels, Bhagwan spoke to people of all professions, castes, religions, and classes. He held discussions with politicians and industrialists, writers and artists, people from the movie industry and students from universities, members of Lion and Rotary clubs, priests and pundits. He spoke to vast audiences consisting of fifty thousand people and to small groups huddled in smokefilled rooms. Bhagwan shares one of his personal experiences of this traveling period:

While I was traveling in India for many years, it used to happen almost every day. People, knowledgeable people, would come— pundits, scholars, learned men—and they would say, "We want to discuss something with you." And my response was always, "If you know, you tell me, share with me. I will be happy and glad to receive it. If you don't know, then I know something. I can share it with you. Then receive it. If we both know then there is no need to talk at all. If we both don't know, what is the point of talking? Discussion is meaningless!"[23]

Beside the fact that Bhagwan's quality of activity (rajas) was being dissipated and spent by all the intense traveling, controversial lectures, discussions, and debates, he also came to realize that he was not making any substantial progress in influencing Indian society. Hence, these travels became less and less meaningful. In Bhagwan's words:

I talked to millions of people in this country; then I had to stop. I was talking to thousands—and in a single meeting [as many as] fifty thousand people. I traveled around this country for fifteen years, from one corner to the other. I simply became tired of the whole thing, because each day I would have to start . . . [with the] ABCs. It was always, ABC, ABC, ABC. And it became absolutely clear that I would never be able to reach XYZ. I had to stop traveling.

Once I was talking on Krishna in a meeting, and people were sitting with their backs toward me, talking with each other. . . . That was the last day, the last straw. In the middle, I left. The president of the meeting said, "Where are you going?" I said, "I am going forever. I am finished with these stupid people. I am talking about Krishna, they have invited me to talk to them, and nobody seems to listen."[24]

Throughout this traveling phase, Bhagwan repeatedly went back to Jabalpur to find a space for himself, to be alone for a while. But that too became more and more difficult. Bhagwan explains:

For fifteen years I also lived like a Jesus, moving in the multitude, and it was impossible to get even a single moment alone. I had to go back again and again to my place where I used to live in Jabalpur, and I kept myself absolutely alone. Jabalpur was very unfortunate. I would go around the country and everywhere I would meet people—but not in Jabalpur. That was my mountain. And when I would come to Bombay, or to Delhi, or to Poona, people would ask me why I . . . traveled . . . back to Jabalpur again and again. Fifteen, twenty days . . . and I would have to go back to Jabalpur for three or four days, and then I would start again. . . . It was unnecessary. I could have gone from Poona to Bombay, from Bombay to Delhi, from Delhi to Amritsar, from Amritsar to Srinagar. Why should I first go to Jabalpur and then again after a few days?

Jabalpur was my mountain. There I kept myself absolutely alone. When it became impossible to be alone even there and the multitude started coming there, then I had to leave that place. . . .[25]

So almost four years after his resignation in 1966 from the university, Bhagwan decided to leave Jabalpur. He cut short his travels, reduced the number of meditation camps, and began packing up his personal library. His friends were eager and ready to find a place for him in Bombay where he could find his own space and also be able to meet people.

He was given a farewell reception on the evening of June 29, 1970, at Shaheed Smarak Bhavan in Jabalpur. The reception was attended by the vice-chancellor of Jabalpur University, journalists, writers, professors, editors of newspapers, and other leading citizens. After all the speeches were made, Bhagwan was asked to speak. He said:

People say that I have become a mahatma [great soul]. In fact, it would be appropriate if you called me a wanderer. Today I am here, tomorrow in Bombay, and the day after I may go to New York. Wherever the divine will takes me, I will follow. I will not forget Jabalpur for this reason also, that I have hurt the feelings of many people. I have been chopping off their erudite talks with my reasoning which has caused wounds. There [in Bombay] I will see that these wounds do not get healed; for I don't want you to sit quietly. I am here to cause wounds, so that you keep thinking. This country never thinks. And remember, the country in which thinking and reflection stops, the race of that country dies. So I will see that as soon as your wounds begin to heal, I will come back again and hit . . . I am not going anywhere [on my own will]. It is up to the divine will. I would like to say only this much: keep thinking. Once the flow of thought stops, the water will turn into a dirty pool, and if it remains flowing, it will be a river.[26]

Bhagwan arrived in Bombay on July 1, 1970. There he began what was a totally new form for him—regular evening discourses with fifty-odd people about spiritual and esoteric matters. He delved into the secrets hidden in various spiritual traditions; he enjoyed answering questions based on the previous lecture and went very deeply into his answers. It was a very intense, live, powerful dialogue, most of which has been compiled and translated from Hindi in *The Mystic Experience.*[27]

Those who were close to him during this period say that his radiance and force were such that one would begin to shake, cry, or feel a lot of energy just by being near him. People felt this very intensely during one of his meditation camps held in August, 1970. He would shake people's beings just by seeing or touching them. He disclosed at this camp that he wanted to initiate into *sannyas* (discipleship)[28] those who felt inwardly connected to him. Thus at a meditation camp held from September 25 to October 5, 1970, at Manali, a beautiful resort in a valley of the Himalayas, Bhagwan initiated six people into sannyas. He gave new names to these individuals and formally began the Neo-Sannyas International Movement.

The main objective of this movement is to create a spiritual awakening all over the world. It aims at eliminating all distinctions and divisions in the name of race, nation, caste, creed, and religion, and building a world family of those who are seeking inner transformation. The Shree Rajneesh Ashram in Poona, the Chidvilas Rajneesh Meditation Center near Antelope, Oregon (now known as Rajneesh Foundation International), over three hundred thousand sannyasins all over the world, and over five hundred meditation centers in India and abroad have grown out of this movement.

The revolutionary concept of neo-sannyas, or Bhagwan's idea of sannyas, can be summarized briefly by the following excerpts from his discourses:

My sannyas is life-affirmative. Nothing like this has ever flowered on the earth. It is a totally new phenomenon. All the old ideas of sannyas were based on escapism, on renunciation. My sannyas has nothing to do with escape. It is against escape, because to me

God and life are synonymous. It has never been said that God and life are synonymous. God has always been put *against* life: you had to drop life to attain God. And I say to you, you have to live as totally as possible, as intensely as possible, as passionately as possible if you want to know God at all.

Each and everybody is there to become a god. That is everybody's destiny. You can delay it, but you cannot destroy it. Giving you sannyas means I am trying to hasten it. Giving you sannyas means I am persuading you not to postpone it any more. Giving you sannyas is nothing but helping you not to delay it any more.

It is out of great respect, because I see the Buddha inside. The Buddha has already waited too long, and you have not looked at it. When I ask you to become a sannyasin, I am saying, "Now the time has come. You take the plunge." Try this new way of life. You have lived in the old way, nothing has happened out of it or whatever has happened has proved only superficial and futile. Try this way too.

The old concept of sannyas all over the world was to give you a rigid discipline, to give you a character, to give you a certain form, a pattern, a lifestyle. My sannyas is not like that at all—it is a radical change. I don't give you any character, because to me the man of character is a dead man. I would like to take all character from you so you are left in a creative chaos . . . so each moment one has to respond to life, not out of a certain pattern.

To respond in the moment without any pattern, just out of spontaneity—whatever the feel of the moment decides to act just like that—is what I call "creative chaos"—a characterless consciousness, a present without past, a freedom unhindered by any discipline.

To live that way is to live the life of a sannyasin. It is utterly beautiful, utterly blessed, but great courage is needed because you don't have a guide, you don't have a particular form, you cannot depend on the past. One has to move from the unknown to the unknown. There is no security in it . . . it is pure adventure.

The older concept of sannyas was very life-negative—it was utterly against life—but my idea or concept is absolutely life-affirmative. Nothing has to be dropped—everything has to be transformed. So this old sannyas was an unholy sannyas: it accepted only part of life—it denied the remaining part. It accepted the mind—it denied the body; it accepted love but it denied sex; it accepted God but it denied the world. And they are all together.

So the old sannyas was an unholy sannyas because it never led anybody to the wholeness of life. It was very perfectionistic. I am not perfectionistic at all. So my sannyas is absolutely life-affirmative. Hence, it is holistic rather than perfectionistic. I am utterly in love with life. It [Bhagwan's sannyas] is non-perfectionistic, it is non-guilt-creating; it does not teach you to condemn anything in you or in anybody else. It makes you more and more aware of all the limitations of life and yet helps you to enjoy with all those limitations.

Let this sannyas be a great love affair with life itself . . . and there is no other God. If you can find life, you have found God. . . .[29]

The initiation into sannyas includes (1) changing one's name, (2) wearing a *mala* (a necklace of 108 beads) which has a locket with Bhagwan's picture framed in it, and (3) wearing clothes of orange or ochre color. Bhagwan has explained in detail the significance of these changes. About the new name he says, "I give you a new name only to make you feel that names are not important. Your old name can simply disappear because it was only a label, it can be changed. You are not the name."[30] A name, even though given to us by others, enters deep into consciousness and we become identified with it, says Bhagwan. But by giving sannyas, Bhagwan destroys this and other identifications as well. He explains:

When you become a sannyasin I want to destroy that identity, because this is the beginning of the destruction of all identities. First I destroy the identity with the name, then I will destroy the identity with the body, then the identity with the mind, then the identity with the heart. When all these identities have been destroyed, you will be able to know who you are: the unidentified, the nameless, the formless, the indefinable.[31]

Pointing out that each color has its own psychology and impact, Bhagwan explains the reason for selecting the ochre color:

One reason is that it makes you feel just like the sunrise in the morning. It is the color of the sun rising; the rays of the sun in the morning are ochre-colored. . . . The color creates a living atmosphere—something alive and vibrating.

So this color was chosen in order that you might vibrate with divinity. You must be alive with divinity; no sadness should have any shelter within you; no sorrow should be allowed to have any shelter. You must be in a dancing mood twenty-four hours. Ochre is dancing color.[32]

Explaining the meaning and significance of the mala, Bhagwan first distinguishes it from the cross. "The mala represents life," he says. "The cross represents death. The mala represents a certain art of making life a garland." Going even deeper into its meaning, he gives this elaborate explanation of the mala and the locket with his picture:

Unless your life knows what eternity is, your life will be just a heap of beads or a heap of flowers, but it will not be a garland; it will not be a mala. It will not have any inner harmony. The beads will remain unrelated. It will be a chaos; it will not be a cosmos. There will be no order, no discipline. But the discipline should be invisible like the thread. . . . The mala represents time as beads, visible, and the thread as eternity, the invisible.[33]

Bhagwan explains further that the 108 beads of the mala represent 108 methods of meditation. One hundred and eight methods of meditation, he says, are the fundamental ones out of which hundreds of other methods can grow. As for his picture in the locket:

. . . The picture is not mine. Had it been mine, I would have hesitated to put it there. . . . The picture only appears to be mine; it is not. No picture of me is possible really. The moment one knows oneself, one knows something that cannot be depicted,

THE EARLY YEARS: SEARCHING

The room where Rajneesh was born

Rajneesh's parents

The house where Rajneesh was born

Rajneesh at fourteen

Rajneesh at seventeen

The temple where Rajneesh meditated

At evening darshan

Sannyasin making malas

Discourse at the ashram

Final blessing to his father

Silent satsang

The tree where Rajneesh had an out-of-body experience

Room at Saugar University

University graduation

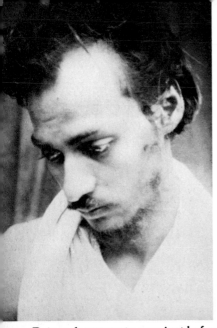
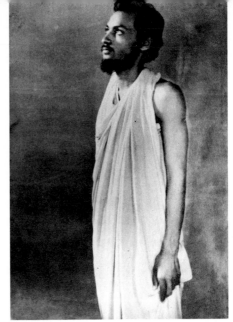

Rajneesh at twenty-one, just before his enlightenment

The tree under which Rajneesh attained enlightenment

THE ENLIGHTENED MASTER

In meditation in Jabalpur, 1963

Discourse at Paktar Hall, Bombay, 1971

Discourse at Cross Maidan, Bombay, 1972

Gate, Shree Rajneesh Ashram,
Poona

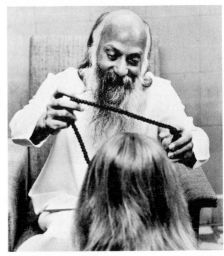

Giving sannyas
to a new disciple

Ma Yoga Vivek and Ma Yoga
Laxmi at darshan

described, framed. I exist as an emptiness that cannot be pictured, that cannot be photographed. That is why I could put the picture there.[34]

In an interview Bhagwan made the following prophetic statement in connection with his initiating people into sannyas:

... the last part of this century, will be very definitive. The latter part of this century will decide the fate of centuries to come. This is going to be a definitive period, definitive in the sense that the belief that human beings are only machines, natural mechanical devices, may become prevalent. If this belief becomes prevalent, it will be difficult to come again to the living current ...

Each day there are fewer and fewer people who know the living current, who know the inner reality, who know consciousness, who know the divine.

This century, the last part of this century, will be decisive. So those who are in any way ready to begin, I will initiate them. If ten thousand are initiated and even one reaches the goal, the trouble is worth taking. ...[35]

As Bhagwan began to attract more and more people and initiate them into sannyas, people started reacting adversely to him. First, those who called themselves "progressive" and "intellectuals" became very unhappy with Bhagwan, for they could not accept Bhagwan as a guru and hence they began to part from his company. In a way, Bhagwan welcomed this situation, since he wanted only those people around him who loved him, who were open to him. He never cared for those who came just to satisfy their intellectual curiosity or to find yet another supporter for their beliefs or ideology. Second, opposition to Bhagwan stemmed from the fact that, with the number of sannyasins increasing around him, he was seen as a potential threat to those in the society whose vested interests Bhagwan had been exposing all along in his country-wide travels and talks. Bhagwan explains:

... They can tolerate a Buddha if he is alone, they know he is alone, so what can they do? They have tolerated Krishnamurti more easily than they can tolerate me. What can Krishnamurti do?

I was also alone, traveling all over the country from one corner to the other corner, almost three weeks every month—on the train, on the plane, continuously traveling. And there was no problem. The day I started sannyas the society became alert. Why? Because to create a Buddhafield, to create a *sangha*,[36] means you are now creating an alternate society. You are no longer a single individual; you are gathering power, you can do something. Now you can create a revolution.[37]

But regardless of negative reaction to him and his sannyas, Bhagwan kept drawing more and more admirers and lovers not only from within the country, but now from the West also. Although between 1968 and 1970 a few seekers from the West had initial contact with him, after he settled down in Bombay more began to approach him. Some English translations of his talks began to appear in the form of booklets.

With the increase in the number of people wanting to see him, it soon became necessary for him to look for a larger place. He moved to Woodland Apartments in December, 1970. Also, he appointed Ma Yoga Laxmi and Swami Yoga Chinmaya as his secretaries. Laxmi was to see to the organizational matters and Chinmaya, who has a very wide and rich experience in yoga and meditation, would conduct classes.

First as Bhagwan's secretary and later as the managing trustee of the Rajneesh Foundation in Poona, Laxmi has been largely instrumental in the expansion and growth of Bhagwan's work. She comes from one of the prominent and well-known Jain families of Bombay. Her father was a very successful businessman and was a member of the Indian National Congress Party. He was close to many leaders of the Congress, including Gandhi, Nehru, and Patel, and he was deeply interested in India's independence movement. But since his children were still young, he helped the movement mainly from the background.

Laxmi also took a very keen interest in Indian politics, especially from 1962 to 1965. She heard Bhagwan for the first time at an All-India Congress Women's Conference— she was then the secretary of the organization. When she saw him, she said something unusual happened: a thrill passed through her body, something clicked; and the next thing that happened was that she began to cry and couldn't hold back. She had never experienced toward anyone such deep feelings of love and reverence before. Later, she and her family became better acquainted with Bhagwan. Had she remained in politics, she might well by now have become a minister at the state level or even in the central government.

In 1969, at a meditation camp held by Bhagwan in a beautiful resort called Nargol, Laxmi had an incredible experience. As she describes it, at this camp Bhagwan gave lectures in the evening and the following morning conducted meditations. In the course of a lecture, Bhagwan said, "You don't know why I have come, but I do!" These words struck the inner chords of Laxmi's heart, and she felt even more deeply for Bhagwan. At night while she lay in her bed, all of a sudden the silent question "Who am I?" started vibrating in her body and it became increasingly intense. Then she broke out in uncontrollable laughter. Her maternal uncle came out from the next room and, seeing Laxmi in that unusual state, became very worried. She had been laughing hysterically. Then Bhagwan came and put his hand on Laxmi's head, and she slowly calmed down. For the entire next day, she was in a state of bliss, but at night again the laughter began. The question "Who am I?" had ceased to vibrate, but the laughter started again. The uncle was assured by now that there was nothing wrong with his niece, although Laxmi kept laughing until morning.

Even though she remained without food and water for three days, her energy did not dissipate. The whole episode brought a sharp awareness in her and changed her life and direction completely. Since that time, she has been working unceasingly under Bhagwan's guidance in giving concrete shape to his vision. Bhagwan once said, "Always remember that Laxmi never does anything on her own. She is a perfect vehicle. That is why she is chosen for this work. . . . Whatever is said, she does."[38]

After this camp, Laxmi often accompanied Bhagwan on his travels. But yet another significant thing happened to her in Bombay while Bhagwan was completing his stay in Jabalpur. One day, in meditation, an ochre color appeared in her vision. When she told her mother about it, her mother said that traditionally that was the color of sannyas. Laxmi said she liked the color so much that henceforth she would wear only clothes of that color. Her mother said it was all right to wear ochre-colored clothes, except that once she chose to wear them, she would have to wear them forever. Laxmi made new clothes in ochre and even attended a women's conference wearing them. It created quite a stir among the delegates attending the conference.

When Bhagwan arrived from Jabalpur on July 1, 1970, his friends gathered to receive him at the railway station. While the train slowly approached, Bhagwan stood at the compartment door greeting people standing on the platform with his customary folded hands. He spotted Laxmi in the crowd wearing her new clothes. As the train stopped, Bhagwan called her and asked in a lighter vein what the change in clothes was about. Laxmi said she could not explain how or why the change occurred. Bhagwan said smilingly, but in a very clear and firm tone, that she was to become his first disciple, the first sannyasin. He named her Ma Yoga Laxmi. Thus, Laxmi became the first sannyasin of Bhagwan, although the official beginning of initiation of others into sannyas occurred several months later at the Manali camp, as has been described earlier.

Bhagwan initiated a few Westerners after moving to the Woodland Apartments, and they started spreading the word about Bhagwan in the West. There are many fascinating stories of how people from the West were drawn to him, but one common factor in their stories is that they recognized Bhagwan as a living Buddha or Christ. After taking sannyas they returned to their respective home countries where they obviously faced opposition, and yet they remained committed to the orange phenomenon. They formed the first close group of Western disciples, and with that a communal life began to develop.

Bhagwan remained in Bombay, and every day the stream of Westerners increased. Slowly and gradually, Bhagwan reduced his public contact, stopped lecturing in open public meetings, and spoke only before small groups at his residence. He stopped giving press interviews and meeting with leading citizens or highly placed people of the society. He traveled very rarely. He now preferred to put his energy into those who were sincere and courageous in their search. He very clearly expressed his wish in letters written in early 1971. Here are a few letters:[39]

1/16/71

My Beloved,
Love!

In the previous birth *I promised many friends that when the truth was found, I would let them know.* I have done so. Hence my travels in India are now over.

Certainly, there are also friends other than the Indians with whom I am building contacts. Although these friends have no idea of the promise—even you do not have—it is still essential that I do what I know has to be done. Henceforth, generally I shall stay in one place. This way I shall be able to pay more attention to the seekers. And thus I shall be of much help to those who are truly in need.[40]

1/16/71

My Beloved,
Love!

My travels are now almost over. *The promises which I made to others in some previous birth, I have kept.* From now on I shall stay in one place. Those who want to come, will come. *They always come.* And perhaps this way I may be of more help to those *who really need me.* I have completed the broader scope of my work. Now I will be doing deeper work. I went and called from one town to another; now I wait for them. This is now the inner command. And I have never done anything different from the inner command, nor can I do it now.[41]

1/16/71

My Beloved,
Love!

Until now, the well reached out to the thirsty [Bhagwan reached out to the seekers], but from now on, this may not be possible. Now the thirsty will have to come to the well. And perhaps this is also according to the law. Is it not? I have almost stopped traveling. The message has been delivered. Now the one who wants to find me will find me, and the one who does not want to find me, I have knocked at his door as well.[42]

2/16/71

My Beloved,
Love!

I am ceasing external travels. But to those who truly call, I will open the doors of inner journey. No, no one will be kept out. I shall enter your heart, and I shall speak to you. And that which you could not understand through outer language, you will be able to follow through inner speech. I have said enough about the subtle through the gross. Now the subtle has to be conveyed through the subtle alone.[43]

In early 1971, a remarkable event took place—Bhagwan's mother received initiation from him and became his disciple. Bhagwan gave her a new name, Ma Amrit Saraswati. Those who were present at the occasion were moved to see the son touching the feet of his mother, and the mother bowing down and touching the feet of her son—now her Master.

When once asked how she felt being Bhagwan's mother, she replied:

. . . two feelings . . . that he is my son, and he is Bhagwan. And so when I bow down to him I feel he is Bhagwan, and at the same time there is a feeling that he is my son; that warmth is there. And that feeling of prayer is also there . . . [that feeling] that he is God.[44]

As his travels and public exposure decreased, Bhagwan was able to see more and more people coming from the West. One of the first to come (from Frankfurt, Germany) was Christine Woolf, who is now known as Ma Yoga Vivek and is the close companion of Bhagwan. She is none other than his girlfriend, Shashi, mentioned earlier in Chapter 3, who had died when Bhagwan was seventeen. Bhagwan revealed the mystery in the following words:

I had a girlfriend when I was young. Then she died. But on her deathbed, she promised me that she would come back. And she has come back. The name of the girlfriend was Shashi. She died in 1947. She was the daughter of a certain doctor, Dr. Sharma, of my village. He is also dead now. And now she has come as Vivek—to take care of me. . . .[45]

Vivek first met Bhagwan at a meditation camp held at Mount Abu in 1971. She came to the meditation camp with a friend and saw for the first time people doing Dynamic Meditation. She recalls:

I saw these people doing the Dynamic and I hid in the bushes. For two days I hid in the bushes! I didn't know what was happening to these people—they were doing all this deep breathing and catharting and the hoo[46] and jumping up and down and laughing and crying and screaming and going naked! I didn't know what it was all about. And then one day, a quite l-a-r-g-e woman came up to me—you know her; it was Taru—and she said, "The Acharya is seeing that you are not doing anything!" And I blurted out, "But I can't do the breathing, I'm really stuck on the breathing; I can't do the breathing . . . " She said "The Acharya wants to see you at three-thirty."

She describes her first encounter with Bhagwan:

So I went to the Circuit House where Bhagwan was staying. I went to the door and I stood at the door, and Bhagwan was sitting on a chair cross-legged with just a *lunghi* on, and he was talking to an Indian. And as he was talking to the Indian he looked at me while I was standing at the door, and my knees buckled, and an Indian standing behind me held me up. I think I must have gone limp.

Then I went in, and Bhagwan said, "Are you having trouble with the meditations?" And I looked at him, and I looked out of the window at the sky. I didn't answer his question. I couldn't. I wanted to, but I couldn't. I just looked at the sky for a few minutes. I don't know what happened but I think I might have passed out for a few minutes because I can't remember what happened in those few minutes. I must have come back from, I don't know, something. He told me how to do the meditations. He told me something else which I don't remember. And that was that.

Another day, Bhagwan was up on the stage, and something happened that night. I wasn't a sannyasin yet. After the meditation, when Bhagwan was going into the car outside, he called me over, because I was just standing on the outside and everyone was just clamoring around him. He called me over and he put his arm around my shoulder and he said, "You're going to live with me." And that was the first time he had ever said anything like that. And when he said it he put his arm around my shoulder and I just leaned against his chest. It felt, it felt like a continuation of something that I had forgotten, that just came right back. And that night I couldn't sleep. I just sat on the balcony, and I knew that "Yes, of course! Yessss . . . " Then I began to relax into the meditations and into the camp.

Vivek had one incredible experience in particular when she cried continually. She sums up her experience of that camp in Abu as follows:

That camp was just explosion after explosion after explosion; every day something happened. I didn't know what was happening, but I just allowed it—everything felt so beautiful, I just let everything come in. And after that particular experience of just crying and crying, of just seeing my mind and seeing my body, after the meditation I just sat there. It was all hilly, all mountainous. And one girl came up to me and asked me what was happening. . . . It was totally beyond anything that I had read or felt. So that was how I started. Then I went back to Bombay and took sannyas.

In answer to a question whether she remembered anything about being with Bhagwan before, Vivek replied:

No, not of being with Bhagwan. A few days after I took sannyas he was giving lectures in English in his room, in his bedroom. There were . . . maybe thirty people. . . . There were so many people and everyone was talking, talking, talking. I was just sitting on the bed. Something went click! It went shoop, shuushh, and I suddenly went *in*. . . . I then had an experience of one past life; it wasn't with Bhagwan. I didn't know anything about past lives.

I didn't know about past lives or reincarnation or anything! I thought the Christian way—you have one life, your only life, and that's it.

In reference to her association with Bhagwan in her past life, Vivek recalled the following conversation between her and Bhagwan:

One of the first things Bhagwan said to me after sannyas was, "Do you remember me? Do you remember anything about me?" And when he said that, again I went click. It goes like a click! . . . Literally everything gets turned inside-out. And the only thing that came out of my mouth was, "I remember that you're someone that I loved very much." I didn't remember then exactly who I was. The only thing that came was he is someone I loved very much. And for me to say that at that time! I was still pretty straight.

He asked me again if I could remember. I just wasn't clear. And that night as I was lying in bed, my death came back, when I died, and the house, and my father. My mother had left. She was something! She had gone off to Pakistan with another man. She left with another man, she fell in love with him. I'm not sure if she left while I was still there or if she left after I died. I think she left before I died. Then the feeling of my death came. Everyone was outside the house sitting on the veranda or in the garden. But Bhagwan was in the room, and I was just with him.

Just before I died, I made him promise that he would call me back, that wherever I was he would bring me back, and I made him promise that he . . . wouldn't go with another woman, that he wouldn't get married! This I don't remember, this is what he told me.

When asked, "He kept his promise?" Vivek replied through tears mixed with joy, laughing, "Yes."

Vivek recalled very clearly the events and places of her past life in Gadarwara:

I remember that the house where we lived was right next to the temple where Bhagwan used to meditate every day. This is how I saw him—he used to go to the temple and I used to see him when I was in the garden or looking out of the window. I used to see him! He says I used to follow him into the temple to annoy him!

Question: And tempt him!

I didn't tempt him. I used to just plainly annoy him. And the temple is situated right on top of a cliff, and there is a river right down below.

Question: Where was this?

In Gadarwara. Where Bhagwan was born.[47] This is a river that Bhagwan often talks about in the lectures, where he used to go swimming. A few times I used to go swimming with him. But usually he just wanted to be by himself. I was a tomboy then, and

Bhagwan says that he used to have to get one friend of his—his name was Shyam—to guard the temple door, "So that Shashi doesn't come in and disturb me anymore!" And I used to bring him food—chapattis and dhal.

Question: To the temple?

Yes. So that after meditating he could eat.

Vivek continued her story by telling how and when she finally came to live with Bhagwan.

Well, when he said that at Mount Abu, he again said it many, many times, "You're going to live with me." And I just kept saying, "When, when, when?" And he would say, "The time is not right." And then one day he said, "Now you come in." I said, "Now?" He said, "Yes!" Just like that. And at first I didn't believe him because I had been waiting for two years.

Question: That long?

Yes. I didn't start living there and start looking after him sort of permanently, you know, doing everything for him, until '73. We moved to Poona in '74, so it must have been in '73 that I totally looked after him and moved in.

When asked whether her whole job since moving in with Bhagwan was to look after him, Vivek said:

Yes, yes. To look after his body. In a way I can see it needs a lot of looking after. In another way it doesn't need *much* looking after, you just have to float with it. I learned that it was much better than worrying myself sick about it which is what I used to do. I used to become so depressed when he became ill but now I have learned to accept what happens to his body and at the same time do the absolute best that I possibly can. It really helps his body if I don't become unhappy about his illnesses. So now I look at the situation and just do everything I can do to help him. When he gets ill, you can't say, "Okay, now what does he have? Give him this medicine." You have to look at what he has, and look at his eyes, look at his face. And then you sort of see, "Well, perhaps this will do." But you can't say that because he has this thing and the doctors say you have to give him that, that you just give him that. So you have to *feel*.

And to the question, "How is it being so consistently close to his energy?" Vivek answered:

The *most beautiful* part—which even now, every day when I see it, it gets more beautiful and more beautiful—is to see Bhagwan sleeping. When he goes to sleep in the afternoon I go after him, so when I come in he's already sleeping. If I'm lucky his face is turned towards me, and . . . that to me is the whole epitome of being with him—to be with him when he's sleeping. It's like he's there and he's not there; like he's a newborn child, like a baby, and at the same time it's like he's a wise old man that's been living eons and eons and has gone through *every* kind of situation and experience, just everything, and yet completely and utterly untouched. He is like a newborn babe, he's also like a very ancient, wise old man. It's like . . . somehow . . . an emptiness lying there, and at the same time a fullness.[48]

The Sanskrit name "Vivek" means "awareness," "consciousness," and it is with constant awareness that she has been looking after Bhagwan, very challenging and yet rewarding task. Bhagwan explained how he gave her this name and what it means. In an interview given on the day Vivek took sannyas, April 16, 1971, Bhagwan said:

Yesterday someone came to me in the morning. I told her to take sannyas. She was bewildered. She said to give her time to think and decide—at least two days. I said to her, "Who knows about two days? You require so long!" I insisted, "Take it today, this moment." But she was not decisive, so I gave her two days. The next morning she comes and takes it. She had not taken two days but only one day. I asked her, "Why? You have been given two days; why have you come so soon?" She said " . . . three o'clock at night, suddenly I was awake, and something went deep within me telling me, 'Go, take sannyas.' " Here it is not a decision that she has made, but a decision that has been made by her deep-rooted mind. But the moment she came in the room, I knew her—that mind which she came to know twenty hours later. So when I say, "Take sannyas," there are so many reasons with every person to whom I say it. Either he has been a sannyasin in his last life, or somewhere in the long journey, he has been a sannyasin.

I had given her another name yesterday, but today I had to change it because I gave her that name in her indecision. Now I am giving her a different name that will be a help to her. But when she came this morning she herself was decided; that name was not needed at all. And I have given her the name Ma Yoga Vivek, because now the decision has come through her *vivek*— her awareness, her consciousness.

Vivek is so close to me that she is constantly on the cross. She has to be; it is difficult. To be so close to me is arduous. The more you are close to me, the more the responsibility [there is]. The more you are close to me, the more you have to transform yourself. The more you feel the unworthiness, the more you start feeling how to become more worthy—and the goal seems almost impossible. And I go on creating many situations. I have to create them because only through friction does integration happen. Only through harder and harder situations does one grow. Growth is not soft, growth is painful.

You ask me, "What do you do with Vivek?"

It is a cross to be with me, and the task is hard.[49]

As Bhagwan cut down the number of travels, speeches, and other outside engagements, his life and work began to take on a totally new form. It was in May, 1971, recalls Swami Yoga Chinmaya, when Bhagwan told him that since the work had gone much deeper, a new dimension had to be given to it. Bhagwan was known until then as "Acharya," which means "teacher." He asked Chinmaya to find a new name for him. Chinmaya suggested a few names, out of which he selected "Bhagwan," which is literally translated as "God." It is a symbolic name, however, and signifies qualities related to heart, love, and devotion. It was meant to symbolize heart-centered work, work that henceforth would happen more in terms of love, in tune with the spirit of Bhakti, Sufism, Tantra. The new dimension that Bhagwan wanted to point out was this dimension of heart or love. His emphasis was no longer on the intel-

lect, on appealing to large numbers of people. The teacher
(Acharya) had communicated enough through the head;
he now wanted communion to take place heart to heart
with those who were in love with him. From then on
Acharya Rajneesh came to be known as Bhagwan Shree
Rajneesh.[50]

Bhagwan narrated the events and significance of this
name change in the following words:

A few years back, one day I called Yoga Chinmaya and told him
to find a new word for me because I was going to function in a
new way. I was known all over the country as the Acharya. The
Acharya means a master, a teacher, and I was a teacher, and I
was teaching and traveling. That was just the introductory part of
my work; that was to invite people.

Once the invitation reached, I stopped traveling. Now, those
who want to, they should come to me. I have gone to their
home, knocked on their doors. I have told them that I am here
and any day the desire arises in them, they can come. I will wait.
I have shown them the path towards me and then one day I
called Yoga Chinmaya and I told him, "Now find a new word for
me because the word teacher will not be enough."

He brought many names for the new function that I was going
to take. . . . I said, "Find something which is universal. Find
something which is not relative." And then he found "Bhagwan."

Bhagwan liked the new word. Pointing out the symbolic
meaning of it, the new dimension of his work, and the
results it brought, Bhagwan continues:

I loved the term. I said, "That will do. At least for a few years it
will do; then we can drop it."

I have chosen it for a specific purpose and it has been serving
well, because people who used to come to me to gather knowledge, they stopped. The day I called myself Bhagwan, they
stopped. It was too much for them, it was too much for their
egos, somebody calling himself Bhagwan. . . . It hurts the
ego.

They stopped. They were coming to me to gather knowledge. Now I've changed my function absolutely. I started working on a different level, in a different dimension. Now I give you being, not knowledge. I was an acharya and they were students; they were learning. Now I am no more a teacher and you are not here as students.

I am here to impart being. I am here to make you awaken. I am not going to give you knowledge, I am going to give you knowing—and that is a totally different dimension.

Calling myself Bhagwan was simply symbolic—that now I have taken a different dimension to work. And it has been tremendously useful. All [the] wrong people automatically disappeared and a totally different quality of people started arriving.

It worked well. Chinmaya's choice was good. It sorted out well, only those who are ready to dissolve with me remained. All others escaped. They created space around me. Otherwise, they were crowding too much, and it was very difficult for the real seekers to come closer to me. The crowds disappeared. The word "Bhagwan" functioned like an atomic explosion. It did well. I am happy that I chose it.[51]

Since the day he adopted the name, he has been asked many times why he calls himself God. What does it mean? And Bhagwan has answered these questions with elaborate explanation. His answers to such questions convey his basic message that everyone is potentially divine, everyone is a potential Buddha. The following is his answer to the questions: "Why do you call yourself Bhagwan? Why do you call yourself God?"

Because I am—and because you are. And because only God is. The choice is not between whether to be a God or not to be a God; the choice is whether to recognize it or not. You can choose not to call, but you cannot choose not to be.

When you call this life God, you bring poetry to it. You bring a vision, you open doors. You say, "More is possible." You say, "We are not the end." Higher realms of possibilities arise in your vision. You start dreaming. The moment you say this existence is divine, dreams become possible. Then you can live a life of adventure. God is the greatest adventure ... the greatest pilgrimage.

There are only two ways to give a label to life. One is the way of the realist—he calls it matter. The other is the way of the poet, the dreamer—he calls it God.

I am an unashamed poet. I'm not a realist. I call myself God. I call you God. I call rocks God, I call trees God, and the clouds God ... with God you can grow, with God you can ride on great tidal waves; you can go to the other shore. God is just a glimpse of your destiny. You give personality to existence.

Then between you and the tree it is not emptiness. Then between you and your beloved it is not emptiness—God is bridging everything. He surrounds you, he is your surround[ing]. He is within and he is without.

When I call myself God, I mean to provoke you, to challenge you. I am simply calling myself God so that you can also gather courage to recognize it. If you can recognize it in me, you have taken the first step to recognizing it in yourself.

It would be very difficult for you to recognize it in yourself, because you have always been taught to condemn yourself. You have always been taught that you are a sinner. Here I am to take all that nonsense away. My insistence is that it is only one thing that is missing in you—the courage to recognize who you are.

... By calling myself God, I am not bringing God down, I am bringing you up. I am taking you for a high journey. I'm simply opening a door towards the Himalayan peaks.

Once you start recognizing that you are also divine, you become unburdened. Then there may be errors, but there are no sins anymore. You are not a sinner. You may be mistaken, you may be wandering on astray paths, but you are not a sinner. Whatever you do, you cannot lose your godhood—that is your nature.

The Indian term for God, Bhagwan, is even better than God. That word is tremendously meaningful. It simply means "the blessed one," nothing else. Bhagwan means "the blessed one" —one who is fortunate enough to recognize his own being.

It has no Christian associations. When you say "God," it

seems as if I have created the world. I deny all responsibility! I have not created this world. I am not that much a fool. The Christian idea of God is one who has created the world. Bhagwan is totally different, it has nothing to do with creating the world. It simply says one who has recognized himself as divine. In that recognition is benediction. In that recognition is blessing. He has become the blessed one.

I call myself Bhagwan because I respect myself. I am tremendously fulfilled as I am. I am the blessed one. I have no discontent. That is the meaning of Bhagwan—when you have no discontent, when each moment of your life is a fulfillment . . . when you don't desire anything in the future; your present is so full, overflowing . . . when there is no hankering.

That's why we call Buddha Bhagwan. He has denied God in his cosmology. He says there is no God, no creator. Christians become very puzzled when Buddha says there is no God, no creator. Then why do Buddhists call him Bhagwan?

Our meaning of Bhagwan is totally different. We call him Buddha, Bhagwan, because he has now no more desires. He is contented. He is happy and at home. He has come home—that is his blessedness. Now there is no conflict between him and existence. He has fallen in accord, in harmonia. Now he and the whole are not two separate things. They vibrate in the same way. He has become part of the orchestra of the whole. And by becoming a part of this great orchestra of stars and trees and flowers and winds and clouds and seas and sands, he has become blessed—we call him Bhagwan.

When I call myself Bhagwan, I am simply saying to you, "Look at me—the roses have bloomed. And what has happened to me can happen to you. So don't feel desperate and don't feel depressed. Look at me and your hope will come back, and you will not feel hopeless."

Calling myself Bhagwan is just a device. I can drop it any day. The moment I see it has started working, the chain has started. The moment I see that now it is no more needed . . . a few people have become a flame; then they will be enough proof. There will be no need to call myself Bhagwan. They will be enough proof. If a few of my sannyasins start blooming, I will drop calling myself Bhagwan. The device will have worked.[52]

During his stay in Bombay Bhagwan became more and more available to individual seekers, to sannyasins, and had increasing contact with seekers from the West. Bhagwan has explained how and why he stopped speaking in public and focused more on individuals.

To talk to disciples is a different matter. To talk to the multitude is a different matter. That is why I had to stop talking to the crowds. I had to create a special class of my own sannyasins with whom I could have a communion of the heart.[53]

In the beginning I was talking to the masses. It was a totally different kind of work: I was in search of disciples. Talking to the masses I was using their language; talking to the masses was talking to a primary class. You can't go very deep; you have to talk superficially. You have to look to whom you are talking.

Then, slowly slowly a few people started turning from students into disciples. Then my approach changed. It was now possible to communicate on higher levels. Now disciples started changing into sannyasins—they started becoming committed, they started becoming involved with me, with my destiny. My life became their style, my being became their being.[54]

Thus, throughout these travels, he quietly found those who were going to become part of his family in the subsequent years. Through his meditation techniques, he was able to gather a number of courageous followers who shared his vision and were eager to explore the new world they only glimpsed. The message was delivered, the path was shown, the distant call to awakening was sounded. Now was the time to sit and watch the stream grow into a river.

As for his drawing more and more Western people, it was clear that he had begun expanding his attention and compassion on a much wider and larger scale—as if he were opening up a huge gate through which the whole world could pass through. Or, he himself had become the gate through which one could find many avenues open for continuing one's own search. Bhagwan was fully aware of the seekers coming to him—the nature, quality, and depth of these seekers. He was also prepared for his forthcoming experiments, in their minute details, for bringing about a transformation in the lives of these seekers.

His years in Bombay, July 1, 1970, to March 20, 1974, were the years of personal and intense encounters with selected individual seekers. He met each individual directly, intimately, face-to-face. During these days, one could get to see him almost any time of the day. He appeared to have started his work with these early disciples—as if he were spreading his roots, as if his roots were searching for a ground to launch a worldwide movement of spiritual awakening.

Of the first few hundred Western seekers who came in touch with Bhagwan, almost ninety percent have remained his lifelong companions. Most of them came to India only as short-term visitors. They came for a short period, stayed around Bhagwan, and then went back to the West to sort out their personal problems and get ready to become a part of Bhagwan's work. They served as mediums through which he traveled around the world—they were like a divine infection that spread Bhagwan's spiritual message all over the world. The hundreds who came in contact with these early initiates came to be with Bhagwan, sooner or later, got involved with him, and became part of his expanding "family."

These early disciples displayed the same qualities that Bhagwan had shown all along—they were very courageous, rebellious, creative, and had great potential for giving birth to a new religious consciousness. The seekers from the West who first came in scores while Bhagwan was in Bombay, and later in thousands after he shifted to Poona, came from different cultural and family backgrounds, religious denominations, and spiritual beliefs, but one thing they had in common: their psyches were ripe and ready to receive Bhagwan's energy and guidance. On the other hand, Bhagwan had also by now begun to unfold his creative energy in devising all sorts of methods, approaches, and experiments that were to be instrumental in bringing about transformation in their lives.

In one of Bhagwan's earlier experiments his Western disciples' will to surrender was put to the test when he sent them to live in a work-farm commune away from Bombay.[55] Swami Anand Veetrag, who came from South Africa to be with Bhagwan in 1973, was made the leader of this group which started with thirty-five sannyasins, male and female. The site was located in the middle of the state of Maharashtra in western India (the same state in which the city of Poona is located). It was a very primitive, rural setting. The nearest village from the farm was half a mile away, the nearest town, Sarli, about six miles, and the nearest city, Chandrapur, about forty-five miles away.

The farm, situated on the river Vanganga, was made available for this experimental work by its owner, Ma Anand Mayi. She is a sannyasin and is recognized by Bhagwan as his mother in a past life. The commune was named Kailash.

The commune and its environment were a real test for these people who were accustomed to independent, affluent lives. They lived out in the field in small huts and had to get along although they came from different countries, different backgrounds, and were not known to each other before. The commune was meant to create a situation where the disciples had to learn how to surrender.

This surrender is different from the Western understanding of surrender. It does not mean submitting to a tyrant or an enemy out of weakness, or giving away one's freedom, body, mind, or belongings to the whim of a leader such as Jim Jones. In the spiritual sense, what is being tested in the disciple is the extent of his or her commitment and ability to submerge or surrender the ego or the ego-attachment to possessions, people, and conditionings in full awareness on the way toward experiencing total freedom and joy.

Surrender in this sense is not dropping out or giving up one's responsibility; rather, it is abandoning one's old beliefs and values and going on a new adventure by surrendering to the vision of life given by an enlightened master who has transcended the ego and become one with the universe. It is only through this kind of surrender that in a spiritual commune there is no longer any work; it is only allowing something to happen through you. The work acquires an aesthetic quality, and a climate is created for everyone to fall in harmony with each other.

At first, the whole thing was chaotic—there was no proper equipment or materials available, no one in the commune knew the native language, and above all, there were no clear guidelines or directions given by Bhagwan. He wanted Swami Veetrag to figure out for himself what needed to be done. "It was scary," confessed the Swami.

The work was hard. It included working in the fields, making bricks, gardening, shopping for supplies in the town. The day began at four in the morning with Dynamic Meditation, followed by housecleaning and then breakfast. The morning chores lasted until ten o'clock. The temperature by then sometimes reached 120 degrees, so during midday the sannyasins kept their bodies cool in the river. At four o'clock they resumed work and stopped at seven in the evening. After supper, there would be either Sufi dance or Whirling Meditation. They went to bed at nine.

As Swami Veetrag put it, "It was like Gurdjieff-style—there was nothing else to do except work, no need to think, work was the main thing. The entire focus was on work with the spirit of surrender. Gurdjieff's 'work' was the main factor that guided or influenced the commune." Commenting on the situation, Veetrag continued, "It was tough, people did react to the conditions strongly; but they also learned how to live in a commune in love and acceptance. Those who could not take it, they left."

The whole experiment was a kind of prototype of what was to unfold later at Poona. The commune lasted for ten months, until August, 1974. When Bhagwan moved to Poona, the commune members began to leave Kailash and gather around the Master at Poona.

When Western sannyasins were sent to communes like Kailash and Samarpan, Indian sannyasins were sent in small groups to different towns and villages. Each of the small groups was called Kirtan Mandali. The sannyasins sang devotional hymns and songs, conducted meditations, and played tapes of Bhagwan's discourses in Hindi. For these sannyasins the experiment was the same—how to surrender, and how to live in love and acceptance under adverse conditions, in an unfamiliar or uncongenial environment. These groups also lasted until Bhagwan moved to Poona.

The intensive traveling of the past years and the poor and irregular eating conditions that were a result began to take their toll. Bhagwan showed signs of poor health; in particular, his diabetes and asthma worsened. It also became evident that a much larger, permanent place was needed. Laxmi was sent out to look for a site suitable for a large ashram. Finally she chose Poona, eighty miles southeast of Bombay, situated on high hills and very well known for its pleasant climate, historic significance, orthodox community, and for its association with enlightened beings, the most recent being Meher Baba. Bhagwan's friends established a public trust, the Rajneesh Foundation, which bought a place spread over about six acres in beautiful and luxurious surroundings on the outskirts of the city of Poona.

Exactly twenty-one years after his enlightenment, Bhagwan arrived in Poona on March 21, 1974, with seven disciples to begin a new phase of his work. The celebration of the anniversary of Bhagwan's enlightenment day and of his arrival took place at 17 Koregaon Park, Poona. The place was named Shree Rajneesh Ashram.

6. Shree Rajneesh Ashram, Poona: A Place of Confluence

BEFORE moving to Poona in March, 1974, Bhagwan indicated that he was entering a new "phase." He explained how the fire of the *rajas guna* and its explosive force had come to an end and the quality of *sattva* had begun:

Now that fire is quenched. Now, just as the sun withdraws its rays in the evening, as a fisherman withdraws his fishing net, I am slowly withdrawing. It is not proper to say that I will withdraw. The withdrawal will automatically happen, because the third phase—that of the sattva guna—has begun. Therefore, you may be watching my gradual withdrawal from activities.[1]

It also seemed that the change of climate had further disrupted his fragile health. His body suffered from acute asthma and it had become very sensitive to allergies. In spite of his delicate health, he continued to hold darshans on the lawn in the mornings. He talked only to those disciples who were either arriving or leaving. The meetings were informal and Bhagwan would sometimes remind his disciples:

... When near me on the lawn, be sincere and true. Don't bring questions which are intellectual. They are useless. Don't bring any metaphysical questions. They are not true; they don't belong to you. Bring your nonsense out, whatever it is. And don't try to manipulate it, don't try to rationalize it and polish it, let it be as raw as possible, because before a Master, you must be naked: you should not wear clothes and you should not hide yourself.[2]

During April, 1974, Bhagwan gave eight discourses[3] on the *Bhagavad Gita* (Chapter 16) in Hindi, in spite of his illness. After the series was over, Bhagwan went into almost complete silence. He did not seem interested in giving further discourses. He also appeared uncomfortable in Poona and astonished everyone by asking that an alternative site be found near Bombay. His plan was that while the ashram in Poona was to remain a meditation center with residential facilities, Bhagwan himself would reside in the alternative site.

Meanwhile, meditations began at a place called the Empress Botanical Gardens, located about three miles from the ashram. The place was found suitable for the two main group meditations: Dynamic Meditation at six o'clock in the morning and Whirling (Sufi) Meditation in the evening.

To everyone's delight, Bhagwan slowly began to recover. He often strolled in the garden and seemed to enjoy the surroundings. It was announced on April 30 that Bhagwan would stay in Poona after all, and the negotiations went ahead to acquire the property adjoining the ashram. There was a new energy, joy, and a sense of direction in the air.

Bhagwan's withdrawal, however, continued, and after June, 1974, he stopped directing meditations in person; instead, an empty chair was brought in and placed on the podium. It marked the beginning of a new phase of his work. The Master was present—but now his disciples had to feel him on a more subtle level. He explained:

One day this physical vehicle has to be dropped. Before it happens you must be ready to work in my absence. And then, even if I am not here in the body, the contact will not be lost.[4]

A typical day for sannyasins in the ashram began with Dynamic Meditation at six o'clock in the morning; the meditation lasted an hour. After meditation sannyasins got ready and assembled to listen to Bhagwan's discourse. Bhagwan arrived in Chuang Tzu auditorium, a part of his residence known as Lao Tzu House, at eight o'clock. While Bhagwan approached the podium, the sannyasins greeted him cheerfully with hands folded in salutation, and Bhagwan returned their greetings smilingly and with folded hands. The discourse lasted for about two hours. The discourses alternated from month to month between English and Hindi. The new series began on the eleventh and ended on the tenth of the following month. After the discourse, sannyasins had breakfast, and from ten-thirty on they busied themselves with assigned jobs, working at least six hours every day of the week. From the eleventh of every month a ten-day meditation camp was held which included five daily group meditations. Visiting sannyasins and non-sannyasins who came from all over the world participated in the meditation camp.[5]

The flow of people coming to the ashram increased steadily, especially people from the West. Several Westerners who had come in contact with Bhagwan in the early 1970s were well-known group therapy leaders; they had now settled down with Bhagwan in Poona. These therapists had given up all the rewards of wealth and prestige that were available to them in Europe and America, because they found in Bhagwan something that was lacking in them—the quality of meditativeness. They came to learn from him how to be meditative. They found him to be the only spiritual master who fully understood the concept of holistic psychology, and the one who could use it as a means of bringing individuals to higher levels of meditativeness.

Some of these well-known therapists were Swami Ananda Teertha, formerly Paul Lowe, founder of Europe's first and biggest growth center, "Quaesitor"; Swami Anand Somendra, formerly Michael Barnett, author of the much acclaimed book *People Not Psychiatry;* and Swami Prem Siddha, formerly Leonard Zunin, a California psychologist and a member of the American Board of Psychiatry and Neurology.

The encounter and primal therapy groups began in April, 1975. Bhagwan has explained the need for therapy in great detail. "Therapy is needed," explains Bhagwan at one point, "because people have forgotten how to be religious. Therapy was not needed in Buddha's time; people naturally knew how to be religious. Therapy is a modern need." And, keeping this need in mind, Bhagwan made it essential for his sannyasins to go through these therapies. "In my commune I have made it a must," he says, "that everybody should pass through therapies. They will help you to unburden the garbage that you have repressed within yourself. They will clean you, and only in a clear, clean heart is prayer possible. And when prayer arises, the miracle has happened."[6]

Some of the groups at the ashram were designed specifically to encourage the exploration of repressed feelings and emotions such as anger, fear, jealousy, greed, and so forth. This constitutes the first stage of the process, the removing of emotional blocks and allowing the energy to flow without impediment. Subsequent to this stage, one can move into more advanced groups that help one's energy to flow through all aspects of one's being: physical, emotional, mental, and transcendent. Essentially, the therapy process, for Bhagwan's sannyasins, is an initial step toward transformation. It is not an end; it is the beginning of the search for ultimate freedom.

Almost all the major branches of holistic psychology were included in the ashram groups: encounter, primal therapy, Reichian therapy, Gestalt, bioenergetics, rolfing, massage, and many other techniques unique to the ashram, designed to work on human energy. Participants in these groups came from almost all over the world and from a variety of different professional backgrounds. The approximately twenty-five thousand who came each year included doctors, lawyers, artists, journalists, businessmen, psychologists, priests, and others who searched for personal transformation through the ashram's group process.

The basic difference between groups that are conducted in the West and those that are held at the Rajneesh Ashram is the presence of Bhagwan as well as his insights into human nature. Swami Anand Rajen, formerly Alan Lowen, who gave up postgraduate research work in psychology at Oxford University, reflects upon this unique characteristic of groups at this ashram:

Good therapists are always on the lookout for someone who understands the human psyche better than they do themselves. In this sense, an enlightened master like Bhagwan is the ultimate therapist. By becoming a sannyasin and practising therapy under his guidance I am allowing him to take me beyond the limits of my previous understanding.[7]

A therapist knows how the mind works, but a master goes beyond mind and touches the deepest core of one's being; hence, a master is not even an "ultimate therapist" —he is far more. The therapists in the West have begun to project themselves as masters, but qualitatively a master and a therapist are two entirely different things. Distinguishing between a master and a therapist, Bhagwan explains:

You are not your surface: you are your depth. Neither the physician nor the therapist can touch that depth. That depth can only be touched by a Master—because he is that depth. A Master is no-mind. And that is the greatest difference that is possible. . . . The Master is a no-mind. He has no know-how. He makes his nothingness available to the disciple, but the nothingness is a healing force. The psychotherapist *tries* to heal, but never succeeds. The Master never tries to heal, but always succeeds. His love is his therapy. . . . Just to be with a Master is to be in a healing presence. The Master is not a therapist, but his presence is therapy. His presence heals, and heals wounds of so many lives. But his process of healing is not psychological: it is existential.[8]

The ashram groups were also unique in that they transcended the usual limits set by society and personality because they functioned in freedom and with greater intensity. The freedom and intensity of these groups, however, have been misunderstood as indulgence and promiscuity, and a great controversy has arisen in regard to these groups, in India and in the West. The controversy has centered more on those groups that help bring out sexual repressions and transform sex energy (according to the tantric tradition) into love, and even higher, into prayer. Bhagwan has spoken of these group experiments:

These are not new experiments. These have been tried by seekers of Tantra for centuries. For ages, Sarahapa and Tilopa and Kanahpa tried it. For the first time, I am trying to give these experiments a scientific base. These experiments were conducted in secrecy for so long. These experiments are described in the scriptures, but the common man was never informed about them because the common man was not considered worthy of respect. I am giving him respect. I ask why the common man should be so ignored. Even he should be given an opportunity to avail himself of these experiments. Why should he not know that there are ways to take his energy upwards? Why should he be deceived? Why should the energy which is dissipated through the sex organs not be given a chance to rise upwards to reach the highest *chakra*, the *sahasrar*, the lotus-flower?

I am revealing that which has been hidden up to now; that is my only offense. For this, I am facing thousands of difficulties. But I am not going to stop these experiments at any cost. I will intensify these and they will reach more and more people. To all those who are willing to listen, who want to understand how life's energy can be transformed from the baser to the higher, these experiments will be made available.[9]

Thus, it is Bhagwan's observation that when one loves naturally, that is, when one accepts his or her senses and emotions—including the baser ones—he or she moves toward transformation. But, he explains further, before this natural state can be attained, one must first see that which is unnatural in him- or herself with courage and honesty. And this is where the groups help. Bhagwan explains this in reply to a question: "Is the purpose of the therapy groups to bring the participant to his or her natural self?"

The purpose of the therapy groups is not to bring the participants to their natural self—not at all. The purpose of the therapy groups is to bring you to the point where you can see your unnaturalness. Nobody can bring you to your natural self; there can be no method, no technique, no device, which can bring you to your natural self—because all that you will do will make you more and more unnatural.

Then what is the purpose of a therapy group? It simply makes you aware of the unnatural patterns that you have evolved in your being. It simply helps you to see the unnaturalness of your life, that's all. Seeing it, it starts disappearing. . . . Seeing the unnatural, you cannot support it any more.

The natural can exist without your cooperation, but the unnatural cannot exist. . . . Once you have seen that it is unnatural, your grip on it becomes loose. Your fist opens of its own accord.

The group is not a device to open your fist. It is just to help you see that what you are doing is unnatural. In that very seeing, the transformation.[10]

On several occasions Bhagwan has been asked why he does not encourage Indians to participate in therapy groups. In reply, Bhagwan points out that the needs of Western people are different from those of Easterners. Also, the psychology of the East differs significantly from Western psychology. He explains:

In the West the psychology that has grown down the ages is extrovert; it is outgoing. The psychology that has been developed in the East is introvert; it is ingoing. For a real Eastern person growth groups are not needed. He needs meditations like *vipass-ana* or *za-zen* in which he can forget the whole outside world and just drown in his own being. He does not need any relationship. Relating is not needed. He needs only to unrelate himself from the world. . . . The growth group is needed because you have a tremendous need to relate, to love, to communicate. In the West the basic problem is how to communicate, how to relate. . . . This is a different psychology. Both are ways to reach the ultimate: one is meditation, another is love. The East has developed the mind for meditation, the West has developed the mind for love. Love means relationship, meditation means non-relationship.[11]

Bhagwan sees a real possibility of going beyond the differences between the East and West. Hence his experiments with groups or with meditations are directed at dissolving those differences and creating a totally new human being—one who will be free of all patterns and conditionings of behavior, Eastern and Western. The only way this can be accomplished is by creating what Bhagwan calls a "meditative space"—this is the ultimate purpose or goal of the therapy groups and the meditations. Bhagwan explains this idea:

The whole goal here is to create a meditative space. How it is created is irrelevant. If you need group processes I will give you group processes, but the meditative space has to be created. If you don't need group processes, if you need simple meditations, I will give you simple meditations, but the meditative space has to be created. Only in that meditative space will the East West disappear, will the Eastern and Western psychology disappear, will the division disappear.

A great experiment is afoot. . . . You may not be aware that something of tremendous import is happening here, something which can become the door to a great synthesis. A great Tao can arise. We can attain to the primordial unity.[12]

After Bhagwan settled down in Poona, his parents visited the ashram occasionally, and although Bhagwan's mother took initiation from him in 1971, as mentioned in the previous chapter, Dadda had not felt spiritually ready until after several experiences of deep meditation. The feeling became intense during one of his visits on October 19, 1975. Dadda describes:

That night I also started meditating from two o'clock. Within fifteen or twenty minutes something very deep happened. Around five o'clock in the morning I heard the soundless sound "OM" coming out of my whole body, and I cried loudly.

Ma [Bhagwan's mother] and Nikalank [a son] woke up and started feeling my pulse. I laughed and said: "Have you gone mad? The moment I have been waiting for a long time has now come." Ma Yoga Laxmi [secretary to the Rajneesh Foundation] came and told the family there was nothing to worry about. Then she told Bhagwan.

Bhagwan came into the room. I asked him to stand in front of me and I touched his feet. Then he touched my feet and I told him: "This is the last time you will be touching my feet, because now I will become your disciple." Bhagwan gave me a *mala* and a new name—Swami Devateerth Bharti. . . . Since that day Babulal is no more there. Everything is changed. All anxieties and worries have disappeared.[13]

It was indeed a rare phenomenon: a father becoming a disciple of his own son. Alluding to his father's initiation, Bhagwan said:

Jesus' father never came to Jesus to be initiated. John the Baptist initiated many, but his own father never came to be initiated. Krishna's father was not a disciple of his. My father is rare—not because he is my father: he is simply rare.[14]

While Bhagwan was bringing peace to the inner world of the seekers coming to him and leading a quiet revolution, outside, the country had slipped into turmoil. India was about to witness its biggest political upheaval since it became independent of British rule in 1947. The political parties who opposed the policies of Mrs. Indira Gandhi and her government united under the leadership of veteran leader Jaya Prakash Narayan (known as J. P.) and mobilized countrywide opposition to Mrs. Gandhi's government. The situation became so critical that Mrs. Gandhi declared a state of emergency at the end of 1975, under which many civil rights were suspended, the press censored, leaders of the opposition imprisoned, and stern measures taken against those who created trouble for Mrs. Gandhi's government. But this subversion of the democratic process resulted in even more agitation and hostility towards Mrs. Gandhi. She faced harsh criticism in the foreign press. The pressure mounted and finally forced her to hold general elections. The public mandate went overwhelmingly against Mrs. Gandhi—she and her party lost the elections, the coalition of opposition parties under the name of the Janata Party achieved a landslide victory. The new Janata Party came into power in the middle of 1977.

Most leaders of the Janata Party and the Janata government were old politicians, conservative and reactionary in attitude, who completely lacked any cohesive vision for the future of the country and were merely driven by their hatred of Mrs. Gandhi. One of the most senior leaders of this party, who also became the prime minister, was Morarji Desai. Desai epitomized a whole generation committed to conservatism and Hindu chauvinism. All through his years in power, Desai harassed Bhagwan and his followers. Revealing the cause of Desai's hostility toward him, Bhagwan said in 1978:

Morarji Desai has been against me all along. The conflict continued at least for fifteen years. . . . Now he is in power, so the fascist in him surfaces. . . . Once, when I started criticizing Mahatma Gandhi, he wanted to prevent my entrance into his province of Gujarat. . . . But he could not do a thing about it . . . and he has held this wound about me in his heart for fifteen years.[15]

Desai carried out a kind of campaign against Bhagwan and the ashram. Because of his strong adherence to Gandhism, his puritanical and orthodox attitude, and his vehement opposition to Bhagwan's views on many controversial issues, he used his influence to create as much trouble as possible for the ashram and the sannyasins. Bhagwan was forthright in his response to Desai's accusations, stating clearly, "My feeling is that he does not understand a bit what is happening here. . . . All he knows is just playing the game of politics. . . . "16

The situation was further exasperated by the Indian press which ran stories about Bhagwan and the ashram that were sensational and mostly inaccurate. Further, the leaders of a number of religious sects also began to criticize Bhagwan and his teachings. Bhagwan responded to all these distortions by explaining the reasons for this negative public reaction, and also his vision and the nature of his work:

With me they're all angry because I am not a hypocrite. I live the way I like to live. I say things that go in tune with my life. For example, I am not against life and its joys—that's what I say, and that's how I live. They would have loved me very much if I was living like a beggar on the surface, if I was starving, naked in the road. . . . I am not an ascetic. I am living herenow [*sic* (here and now)] in paradise. And I teach you also to live herenow in paradise: this very earth the paradise, this very body the Buddha.

I am teaching my people to live a single, unitary life. . . . Be natural. I want Buddha, Gautam the Buddha, and Zorba the Greek to come closer and closer—to become one. My sannyasin has to be "Zorba the Buddha."

I am a materialist-spiritualist. That is their trouble. They cannot conceive of it. They have always thought that materialism is something diametrically against, opposite, to spiritualism. And I am trying to bring them closer. In fact, that is how it is. Your body is not opposed to your soul; otherwise, why should they be together? And God is not opposed to the world; otherwise, why should he create it?

That's my whole work here, and I can understand why Morarji [Desai] strongly dislikes it. He is a traditionalist, an orthodox Hindu, with no vision, with no insight into life. He is just a fascist

Hindu, and my approach toward life is that of individual freedom —utter freedom for the individual.

The individual should not be interfered with unless he becomes dangerous to other people. . . . Each individual has to be himself and has to be given space enough to be himself.

That the fascist mind cannot allow.[17]

While Desai and his Janata government remained in power, bureaucratic obstacles prevented the ashram's efforts to buy land where a new commune could be established according to Bhagwan's vision. The Indian government also instructed its foreign embassies to deny visas to anyone who wanted to visit the Rajneesh Ashram in Poona. Furthermore, the government also denied permission to television and film companies from England, Italy, Germany, Canada, and the United States to film the activities at Shree Rajneesh Ashram. The BBC in London was one of these. Their application was turned down in April, 1978. A senior spokesman for the BBC said in his letter to the Rajneesh Foundation:

It's incredible to me that after all the protestations we had about a free press and allowing journalists access to anything they wanted in India, that the first time we put in an application for something as unpolitical as the Ashram, we get held up.[18]

In August, 1978, L. K. Advani, Minister for Information and Broadcasting, made a public statement in the Rajya Sabha (the Upper House of the parliament). He stated that the ban had been imposed on all foreign films and television companies because "it is felt that a film of the ashram would not reflect favorably on India's image abroad."[19] Referring to Advani's statement, Bhagwan invited the Janata government to set up a commission and discover what might be happening in the ashram that would not "reflect favorably on India's image abroad." He also invited Advani to visit the ashram personally and see for himself what went on. Neither invitation was taken up. The evidence of

discrimination against the ashram by the Janata government was overwhelming. It became evident that the very
people who had criticized and opposed Mrs. Gandhi for
suppressing democratic rights, and who came into power
by pledging publicly to support democracy, secularism, and
free press, were themselves engaging in these practices
where Bhagwan and the Rajneesh Ashram were concerned.

Regardless of how the world outside treated Bhagwan
and the ashram, activities in the ashram moved along well,
growth continued, and more and more people came to
Bhagwan. Bhagwan's daily schedule included his meeting
at evening darshan with a small group of ashram sannyasins, sannyasins visiting from other parts of India and from
abroad, and occasionally non-sannyasin visitors. These
darshans provided intimate communion with the Master,
who gave sannyas and explained the meanings of the new
names; he chatted with sannyasins who had either arrived
or were returning to their homes, talked with individuals in
a friendly and compassionate way, and helped them if they
had any problems or questions.

Later, after February, 1979, these darshans were given a
new form and dimension. They were called "energy darshans" and the format was changed. Instead of responding
directly to the problems or questions of sannyasins in darshan, Bhagwan would send his replies through Ma Yoga
Laxmi after reading letters from the sannyasins. The giving
of sannyas remained as before except that now Bhagwan
went into more elaborate detail when explaining the meaning of the new name. The arrival and departure darshans
were changed to "blessing darshans," in which there was
no conversation with Bhagwan; Bhagwan would press his
thumb or forefingers in the center of the forehead (also
known as the "third eye") of the sannyasin who closed his
or her eyes as energy was received from the Master. After
the "blessing darshan," sannyasins, especially the regular

ashram workers, received an even more intense experience of energy and ecstasy. During this part the atmosphere was filled with joy and festivity. While Bhagwan pressed the "third eye" of the sannyasin, other sannyasins danced ecstatically around him in a semicircle and the group swayed to the music. The whole experience was like opening out or being totally receptive to the flow of energy. Bhagwan describes the phenomenon:

Whenever a Master wants to help you, to cleanse your energy channel, your passage, if it is blocked, he simply possesses you. He simply descends into you, and his energy, which is of a higher quality, purer, unbounded, moves in your energy channels. . . . If a disciple is really surrendered, the Master can possess him immediately.

And once you are possessed by the energy of the Master, once his *prana* [energy] surrounds you, enters you, much is done very easily which you cannot do in years. . . . But if a Master can enter in you like a waterfall, many things are simply washed away. And when the Master has gone out of you, suddenly you start to be a totally different person—cleaner, younger, vital . . . [20]

In June, 1979, Bhagwan's health, which had been fairly good since he arrived from Bombay, gave way, and Bhagwan had to stop giving discourses and darshans. Sannyasins participated in a silent music meditation with him in Buddha Hall from June 11 to 20, 1979.

Bhagwan did not speak, as his body was not well. He rested for a few days—there were no lectures and no evening darshan— and by the third day all was well. Still, he did not come to speak. The hall was filled with expectant disciples enjoying music that was there as part of the meditation on Bhagwan's absence. At the front of the lecture hall was his poignantly empty chair.

On the fourth day Bhagwan came, a fragile, gentle breath of love floating into the lecture hall, onto the dais, into the chair, accentuating the empty space with his emptiness.

We hummed, we swayed, we sat and tasted his nectar pouring on us, generous and abundant, like the monsoon rains outside.

By the ninth day the energy had mounted to a crescendo in his eloquent presence. It is as if he were entering each of us, feeling and sensing who could be with him without the need of words, either outer words or inner words.

On the tenth day, a few thousand disciples gathered in the hall with Bhagwan to celebrate ten days of silence. He was there, before us, pure essence, a hand poised in midair, exquisite in its enlightenment; dancing, twirling orange-red flames around the periphery, the longing of thousands of winged hearts suffused the very air with prayer.

Movement from words to sound and rhythm, sound to silence, alive silence, pure pure energy-space.[21]

It was a very beautiful experience for the disciples, although they could not help but worry about the Master's health. They felt him even more intensely, lovingly, and prayerfully. Bhagwan recovered from the illness and resumed his morning discourse on June 21. He spoke to the disciples that morning quite intimately and more specifically about himself. He talked elaborately on silence, on the value of sitting in a silent communion with him, and gave a hint of the fact that he might stop talking in the near future. (He did stop talking about two years later, an account of which is given in the following chapter.) The following excerpts are from the discourse of June 21, 1979:

The time is ripe, the time has come for it. My whole work here consists in creating a Buddhafield, an energy-field where these eternal truths can be uttered again. It is a rare opportunity. Only once in a while, after centuries, such an opportunity exists ... don't miss it. Be very alert, mindful: listen to these words not only by your head but by your heart, by your every fiber of being. Let your totality be stirred by them.

And after these ten days of silence, it is exactly the right moment to bring Buddha back, to make him alive again among you, to let the winds of Buddha pass through you. Yes, he can be called back again, because nobody ever disappears. Buddha is no more an embodied person; certainly he does not exist as an individual anywhere—but his essence, his soul, is part of the cosmic soul now.

I am immensely glad, because after these ten days of silence I can say to you that many of you are now ready to commune with me in silence. That is the ultimate in communication. Words are inadequate; words say, but only partially. Silence communes totally.

And to use words is a dangerous game too, because my meaning will remain with me, only the word will reach to you—and you will give it your own meaning, your own color. It will not contain the same truth that it was meant to contain. It will contain something else, something far poorer. It will contain your meaning, not my meaning. You can distort language—in fact it is almost impossible to avoid distortion—but you cannot distort silence. Either you understand or you don't understand.

And for those ten days, there were only two categories of people here: those who understood and those who did not. But there was not a single person who misunderstood. You cannot misunderstand silence—that's the beauty of silence. The demarcation is absolute: either you understand or you simply don't understand—there is nothing to misunderstand.

These ten days have been of strange beauty, and of a mysterious majesty too. I no more really belong to this shore. My ship has been waiting for me for a long time—I should have gone. It is a miracle that I am in the body still. The whole credit goes to you—to your love, to your prayers, to your longing. You would like me to linger a little while longer on this shore, hence the impossible has become possible.

These ten days, I was not feeling together with my body. I was feeling very uprooted, dislocated. So it was strange to be in the body when you don't feel that you are in the body. And it was also strange to go on living in a place which no more belongs to you—my home is on the other shore. And the call comes persistently! But because you need me, it is out of the compassion of the universe—you can call it God's compassion—that He is allowing me to be in the body a little more.

Words are becoming more and more difficult for me. They are becoming more and more an effort. I have to say something, so I go on saying something to you. But I would like you to get ready as soon as possible so that we can simply sit in silence . . .

listening to the birds and their songs, or listening just to your own heartbeat. Just being here, doing nothing.

Get ready as soon as possible, because I may stop speaking any day. And let the news be spread to all nooks and corners of the world: those who want to understand me only through words, they should come soon, because I may cease speaking *any* day. Unpredictably, any day, it may happen—it may happen even in the middle of a sentence. Then I am not going to complete the sentence! Then it will hang forever and forever . . . incomplete.

But this time you have pulled me back.[22]

While sannyasins enjoyed energy darshans, living in celebration, and working creatively, they were unaware that an experience of great intensity and meaning was to occur shortly—the death of Bhagwan's father, Dadda.

Dadda and most of the family, including Bhagwan's mother, brothers, and their wives and children, had left Gadarwara and had been living at the ashram since 1978. It was almost impossible not to notice Dadda—the white-haired man who was old in body but whose face showed vitality and joy. His bright and laughing eyes showed inner peace and contentment. He was a delightful host during the *kirtan*[23] celebrations that were held every week at his residence.

Dadda had not been in good health for some time. He had had six heart attacks since 1975, and was admitted to the hospital for heart failure about a month and a half before he left his body. The following is a personal account of how I experienced the incident.

It was one of those damp evenings of the monsoon season. I was working in my office after supper. I had been working half an hour when I heard a female voice: "Swami, Dadda is dead. We are going to have a celebration in Buddha Hall." The message came like a jolt. I looked at the door to see who she was, but she had left. I immediately put aside my papers, got up, and joined other sannyasins in the Buddha Hall. The news cut me off from everything else; it just pushed me into the moment, and I remained seated silently in Buddha Hall.

Just a week before I had met with Dadda in his hospital room. I had an appointment with him. In fact, it was agreed that we would talk about Bhagwan and he would tell me stories, incidents from Bhagwan's childhood. He looked as cheerful as ever and also seemed to have greatly recovered from an attack of paralysis. He had now been hospitalized for about five weeks. Doctors had assured his release within the next few days. But as I sat, touching his feet, he looked at me and said apologetically:

I don't feel like saying anything more than what has already been said previously by me [about Bhagwan]. I don't like to see people anymore. I don't even feel like eating anymore. I feel sorry for this, since you have come from such a long distance especially for this.

I told him not to feel sorry, and said that we could arrange a meeting later when he was back at the ashram and had fully recovered. I chatted briefly with Ammaji (Bhagwan's mother) and Shailendra and Amit (Bhagwan's brothers). With the help of his sons, Dadda walked slowly from the room, feeling very hot and exhausted. We brought him back to the room and laid him down on the bed. He closed his eyes and went to sleep. I returned to the ashram.

Dadda died on September 8, 1979, at 8:45 P.M. But this was the death of his physical body. He had attained the state of *samadhi,* the state of detachment of mind from body, early that day at three o'clock in the morning. And with that first glimpse of the eternal he became aware that he was going to die. He sent a message for Bhagwan to come, he wished to say goodbye to him. However, immediately thereafter he sent another message that Bhagwan need not bother, he did not have to come. Bhagwan went to see his father anyway. The next morning, replying to Vivek's question in his lecture, he described his meeting with his father:

Yesterday I went to see him. I was immensely happy that now he can die a right death. He was no longer concerned with the body. The other two times I had gone on my own. Yesterday he called me to come, because he was certain that he was going to die. He wanted to say goodbye and he said it beautifully, with no tears in his eyes, with no longing for life anymore.

Once this attachment to the body, to life, is gone, one becomes free from the cycle of birth and death. With no desire left to come back in the body, to finish the unfinished desires, consciousness becomes free to merge into the eternal. "Hence, in a way," says Bhagwan,

it is not a death but a birth into eternity. Or it is a total death, total in the sense that now he will not be coming any more. And that is the ultimate achievement. There is nothing higher to it . . . higher than it.[24]

This death was extraordinary, but then again so was the meeting of father and son, the Master and disciple. Two beings—one already one with the whole and the other stepping into it. It was their last meeting. The father had loved his son immensely. Bhagwan had served him lovingly since childhood. At one of my meetings with Dadda, he remembered fondly how once during an illness Bhagwan, when he was fifteen, used to give him a massage and, despite the doctor's prohibition, bring candies to him secretly and feed him. But now this illness was the last one, and father and son were no longer the same. It was an incredible meeting of two beings in an intimate yet unattached relationship.

Bhagwan gave a further glimpse of their last meeting in one of his Hindi lectures:

On the last day he sent a message, right in the morning, so I said, "I am coming." When I sent the message that I was coming, he immediately informed me that now there was no need, don't bother. Yet I went at three o'clock. I was happy, because his attachment to me, his attachment to seeing me, that last bondage had been broken. And when I told him that his room was ready, a new bathroom had been built, now in a day or two he would be released from the hospital; a new car had been called for him—since his leg hurt it would be difficult for him to walk, so a new car had arrived. Having heard all this, he did not take any interest in the new car, nor in the new room, nor in the new bathroom; he only shrugged his shoulders, didn't say a thing. Had he shown a little interest he would have had to return. I was happy when he shrugged his shoulders. His shrugging shoulders meant that everything was meaningless—now all the houses were meaningless, all cars were meaningless. Now there was neither coming nor going.[25]

So a great celebration began in Buddha Hall at about nine that evening. Disciples were crying, dancing, and singing "Hallelujah." That is the way Bhagwan wanted it to be. Because, as he said,

He left the world in utter silence, in joy, in peace. He left the world like a lotus flower. It was worth celebration. And these are the occasions for you to learn how to live and how to die. Each death should be a celebration—but it can be a celebration only if it leads you to higher planes of existence.

More sannyasins began to congregate in the hall. I was going deeper within myself as the dancing and singing became more and more intense.

Around ten-thirty Dadda's body was brought into the hall and laid on a marble stage from where Bhagwan gave his discourses. Bhagwan's mother and other family members, full of tears, were near the body. There was a distinct glow on Dadda's face and he looked to me more as though he were deep in meditation, rather than dead. After a while, Bhagwan came. As usual he smiled and signaled greetings to everyone with hands pressed together. Then he placed a garland of leaves around Dadda's neck and knelt down. It was a remarkable scene; the energy in the hall was intense. Bhagwan touched his father's head in two spots. In the lecture, he explained what he was doing:

I had touched his body in two spots—one on the *Agya chakra* because there were only two possibilities—either he could have left his body through the *Agya chakra,* in which case he would have had to take one more birth, only once. And if he had left through the seventh chakra, *Sahasrar,* then he would not have to take birth again. First I checked his *Agya chakra.* I put my hand on his *Agya chakra* with a little concern because the chakra through which life departs opens up like a bud blossoms into a flower. And those who have experience of *chakras* can immediately feel, just by touching, from where life found its way out. I was very happy to see that his life had not passed through the *Agya chakra.* Then I touched his *Sahasrar,* which is also known as the "thousand petal lotus," and found it open. He flew away through the seventh door.[26]

In a few minutes Bhagwan left the hall smiling, and a little after that the body was taken to the nearest cremation ground, followed by the hundreds of saffron-robed sannyasins chanting, "Rejoice, rejoice!" Around two o'clock in the morning the body was placed on the pyre and the fire was lit. As the chanting and dancing reached its peak, the orange-colored flames engulfed the body and the whole cremation ground turned orange.

Bhagwan has spoken in as much detail on death and on many of its dimensions as he has on life and its many facets. His main concern in speaking on death has been to make his disciples understand the phenomenon and use it as a means of maturing their perception of life itself. His revelation of the deep mysteries of death is essentially based on his own direct experience of the deepest meanings of death and not merely an intellectual conceptualization of it. The very reason why death has remained an enigma in the West seems to be that the people have never encountered death without attempting to interpret it through their minds. In fact, the entire Western attitude toward death has been one of negative acceptance. Death is taken as the end of life, a reality recognized as inevitable, yet braved with fear and accepted only reluctantly. The only way to face it has been to avoid it, to escape from it by looking at it intellectually. People of the West see death as an object not only separate from life, but in opposition to it.

Death is fundamentally a part of life. Death is not somewhere in the future; it coexists with every living moment. Hence, for Bhagwan, death is not an intellectual, but an "existential" problem. He says:

You cannot solve it by thinking. You can create only fake solutions. . . . Death is there: face, encounter, be with this situation totally. Don't think about it. What can you think? The death is such a new phenomenon, it is so unknown, that your knowledge is not going to help in any way, so put aside your mind.[27]

Based on his own experience, Bhagwan points out another dimension of death—"the dimension of meditation." He explains:

Sadness will be there, sorrow will be there, a heavy burden will be on you—let it be there. It is part—part of life, and part of maturity, and part of the ultimate realization. Remain with it, totally present. This will be meditation and you will come to a deep understanding of death. . . . Then death will take you to the very center of life—because death is the very center of life. It is not against life; it is the very process of life.[28]

Bhagwan has put most emphasis on the kind of death that leads one toward eternal life; as the *Upanishads* say, *"Mrityorma Amritam Gamaya"*—Lead me from death to immortality. "I am asking you," Bhagwan says,

to live in awareness. Live in such awareness that you remain conscious even in death, then even your death is reached in meditation, then you continue to be wakeful and death happens.

The lamp of consciousness should be kept burning while you are being freed from the body. If only you can die consciously, you will never be born again or die again. Then you will reach the eternal.[29]

Dadda indeed met a conscious death. It was a beautiful death, a total death. This was possible because he had lived life fully, with joy and laughter. He knew life, of course, but he did not know that his own son would one day teach him what death was all about—the kind of death that would bring him eternal peace and enlightenment.

Celebrating life and death in the same spirit, the ashram continued to grow. More and more creative activities were added to the ashram. For the disciples, creativity and artistic expression became an integral part of their daily meditation.

To Bhagwan's disciples, sannyas meant living in the world without being attached to it and sharing the bliss of meditation with others through creating beautiful arts and crafts. Hence, many different kinds of arts and crafts flourished at Shree Rejneesh Ashram. The ashram pottery acquired a considerable reputation. The weaving studio became equally well known and produced a wide range of ponchos, jackets, shawls, blankets, and children's toys. Dresses and robes designed and manufactured at the ashram became very popular.

The Rajneesh Theatre Group won critical acclaim from the Indian press with its colorful production of Shakespeare's delightful comedy, *A Midsummer Night's Dream* in July, 1979, at Bombay. The group also toured other cities in India, Surat and Ahmedabad in the state of Gujarat. Encouraged by its continued success, the group presented *A Midsummer Night's Dream* and *Twelfth Night* in New Delhi in March, 1980.

The ashram's health center was equipped with a modern laboratory and surgical facilities, and staffed by qualified doctors. The staff of the health center carried out extensive research in controlling such indigenous diseases as hepatitis, which especially affected people coming from the West.

The tape department used highly sophisticated instrumentation to record Bhagwan's daily discourses. It was run by sannyasin electronic engineers. Sannyasins also experimented with new ways of utilizing power, including the construction of houses fitted with solar heating panels.

The ashram also produced detergents and soaps that were not detrimental to plant life when recycled into the environment. It manufactured a wide range of soaps, shampoos and creams, based on nonanimal fats and natural oils. In the canteen, a wide range of excellent vegetarian food was always available, including eggless cakes and pastries, homemade curd, cheese, and peanut butter.

The sannyasins also showed a remarkable achievement in the area of hydroponics.

By 1979, more than one hundred therapy groups were being conducted within the Department of Psychology of the emerging Rajneesh International Meditation University.[30] These groups were later consolidated into twenty major groups, residential and nonresidential. In addition, a variety of special classes were held: Tai Chi, karate, Indian dance, English and Hindi language, and chamber music.

It soon became impossible for this rapidly expanding experiment in communal living to be contained within the six acres of land at Shree Rajneesh Ashram in Poona. Efforts were intensified to acquire four hundred acres of largely barren land, twenty miles from Poona, in a valley known as Jadhavwadi, in a town called Saswad. Plans were made to build the "Rajneesh Neo-Sannyas International Commune" here, where ten thousand sannyasins could live and work together in love and meditation as a self-contained, self-sufficient community.

The process of acquiring the place began by leasing an old castle adjoining the property in order to house handicraft industries and residential therapy groups. Also, the ashram sannyasins began cultivating some of the land. Efforts were made to get permission from the Maharashtra State Government to use part of the land for nonagricultural purposes.

The new commune at Jadhavwadi was inaugurated on December 11, 1979—Bhagwan's forty-eighth birthday. Over six thousand sannyasins and visitors drove out to the site in a convoy of buses, cars, and motorbikes. At the highest spot of the property, the specially designed flag of "Rajneeshdham" was raised. This spot was to be saved for building a beautiful meditation temple. Forty-nine different departments of the new commune were announced. The plan included meditation halls, therapy chambers, a university, a five-star hotel, a cinema and film institute, colleges of dramatic art, crafts, music, dance, painting and sculpture, and many other facilities.[31]

Bhagwan's vision sees a commune as a framework within which its members can experience spiritual awakening. The commune and its environment, which Bhagwan calls a "Buddhafield," would allow things to be done in a relaxed, creative, and loving way. There would no longer be any work, in its literal sense. Rather, the whole idea would be to foster spiritual growth by allowing individuals to be open to change. This way, the work would no longer be serious business; instead, it would become continuous play (*leela*). In this way communal life would acquire an aesthetic quality. In this commune no one would function in a stereotyped, established role or position; each person, instead, would be seen as having undiscovered potential and would be provided opportunities to discover his or her divinity. The commune would be more of a laboratory than an organization, where experiments would be carried on to see which method, path, technique, or insight could best bring Buddhahood to the earth.

Bhagwan has described his vision of the commune in

detail, explaining how the commune would give birth to a new individual of the future, and how it could turn this earth into a paradise. The following excerpts summarize his vision:

This is the meaning of a church, a commune; we pool our consciousness in one space, and then each affects the other. Then great energy is released. Alone, you cannot go very high. Alone, you are alone. Alone, you have all kinds of limitations. When you are one with many, infinite energy is available. And many things will start happening which cannot happen alone.

You are pooling your energies with me. And naturally, you will start feeling the same kind of rhythm, the same moods passing through the whole commune.

And this whole experiment is to bring a kind of Buddhahood into the world. This commune is not an ordinary commune. This is an experiment to provoke God. You may not be aware of what is going to happen. You may be aware only of your problems. You may have come to me only to solve your problems. That is secondary; I am cooking something else.

I am trying to create a space where God can descend more and more. This commune will become a connection. The world has lost that connection; God is no longer a reality. As far as this century is concerned, Nietzsche is right to say that God is dead. The connection is broken. God can only exist through the connection. God will be there, we are here, but there is no bridge. So how do we know? This commune is an experiment to create the bridge. . . .

I am working slowly—slowly I am adding more people to your commune. Soon there will be thousands. I want to create a small city, sooner or later, where people will be living totally egolessly. And the more people there are, the greater the possibility for happenings, for miracles—because the more God will be available. The sky will come closer to you.

When you join me as a sannyasin, you are dropping yourself, disappearing. When you join the commune then you have to utterly efface yourself. If a little bit is hanging there then you will be a trouble to yourself and to the commune too. And you will not be benefitted by me.

The new commune is an experiment in spiritual communism.

The word "communism" comes from "commune." There is only one possibility of communism in the world, and that possibility is through meditation.

Communism is not possible through changing the economic structures of societies. The change of the economic structures of societies will only bring new classes; it cannot bring a classless society. The proletariat may disappear, the bourgeoisie may go, but then there is the ruler and the ruled. That's what has happened in Russia; that's what has happened in China: new distinctions, new classes have arisen. Communism is basically a spiritual vision. It is not a question of changing the economic structure of the society, but of changing people's spiritual vision.

The new commune is going to be a space where we can create human beings who are not obsessed with comparison, who are not obsessed with the ego, who are not obsessed with the personality. The new commune is going to be a context in which a new kind of man can become possible. Socrates says that the Master is a midwife, and he is right. All Masters are midwives: they always bring new humanities into existence. Through them a new man is born.

The old man is finished. The old man is no longer valid. And with the old man, all that belonged to the old man has also become invalid, irrelevant. The old man was life-negative. The new commune will create a life-affirming religiousness. The motto of the new commune is: This very body, the Buddha; this very earth, the Lotus Paradise.

My effort in the new commune is to create a man who is not partial, but who is total, whole, holy. A man should be all three together. He should be as accurate and objective as a scientist, and he should be as sensitive, as full of heart as the poet, and he should be as rooted deep down in his being as the mystic. He should not choose, he should allow all these three dimensions to exist together.

The new commune is going to create a space, a context, for this multidimensional human being to be born. And the future belongs to this new man.

The new commune is going to be a totally new kind of religiousness, spirituality. Nobody is going to be a Hindu or a Chris-

tian or a Moslem or a Jain, but everybody is going to be religious
—just religious. To me, religion needs no adjectives—and the
moment a religion becomes attached to an adjective it is no longer religion, it becomes politics.

The new commune will not respect any masochistic tendencies. It will not respect any asceticism; it will not respect any ab-
normal, unnatural tendencies—it will respect the natural man. It
will respect the child in man; it will respect innocence. And it will
respect creativity. It will respect a man who paints a beautiful
picture; it will respect the man who plays beautifully on the flute.
The flute player will be religious, and the painter will be religious,
and the dancer will be religious, not the man who goes on long
fasts, who tortures his body, who lies down on a bed of thorns,
who cripples himself.

It is going to be the beginning of a new humanity. It is needed,
absolutely needed. If we cannot create the new man in the coming twenty years, by the end of this century, then humanity has
no future. The old man has come to the end of his tether. The
old man is ready to commit global suicide. The third world war is
going to be global suicide; it can be avoided only if a new kind of
man can be created.[32]

While the ashram was moving ahead in the new energy
generated by the inauguration of Rajneeshdham and while
it got busy planning the new commune, the country was
filled with the excitement of upcoming general elections.
The elections were especially significant because Mrs.
Gandhi, who was thrown out of power by the Janata Party
earlier, was determined to contest the elections and win.
She assembled her party and succeeded in convincing the
people how the Janata government had performed ineffec-
tively and inefficiently since it came to power in 1977.

Bhagwan gave his blessings to Mrs. Gandhi and
expressed his happiness at her return.

Once she is back in Parliament she will not be out of power for
very long. She is India's only ray of hope because she has guts,
she can get things done.

Bhagwan's assessment of Mrs. Gandhi was clear and forthright:

She has the courage to take revolutionary steps which are urgently needed. . . . Indira [Mrs. Gandhi] has always liked my thoughts; she has always had a kind of love for my way of thinking. I want this country to go through a great revolution, and Indira is capable of it. She has all my blessings.[33]

Mrs. Gandhi won the elections, her Congress Party won the majority in Parliament. She and her party came back to power in January, 1980, after an absence of merely three years.

Bhagwan continued to sharply criticize the vested interests, the orthodox religions, and the hypocritical leaders of the society—whether of the East or the West. As we have seen, his sole concern has always been to see things as they are and reveal the truth regardless of how anyone else feels about it. Because of this, he has invited trouble and opposition from every direction. The most violent and dramatic reaction to his discourses and work, however, occurred on May 22, 1980, when a religious fanatic attempted to assassinate Bhagwan during his morning discourse.

The ashram day began as usual on May 22. Bhagwan was then speaking in Hindi. About fifteen hundred people had gathered in Buddha Hall on the pleasant summer morning and were listening to Bhagwan's discourse. Suddenly, at about eight-thirty, a young man stood up in the audience and started running toward Bhagwan, shouting something in Hindi, which translated into English meant, "Bhagwan Rajneesh, you are speaking against our religion, we won't tolerate it." His path was immediately blocked by the ashram guards, but before they could seize him he managed to throw a large knife that passed in front of Bhagwan and landed on the concrete floor of the hall.

Minutes before this incident, the ashram security had received a tip-off from the Poona police that an attack was imminent. While the attack was happening, a police squad arrived at the ashram gate. The assailant, who was later identified as Vilas Vitthal Tupe, a member of an extreme Hindu organization based in Poona, was gently apprehended by the guards, removed from the hall in silence, and handed over to the police. A wave of shock passed through the sannyasins sitting in the hall, but there was no panic.

Bhagwan remained seated throughout the attack—calm and cool, absolutely unperturbed. In fact, he calmed the audience, saying, "Remain seated, please remain seated in your place ... don't worry ... be seated ... ," and he continued his discourse:

Do you see what kind of utility these scriptures have? Now this poor man has no idea what he is doing. He is unconscious. He is not in his senses. He thinks he is protecting the religion. Religion protects you, or you protect the religion? He thinks in terms of "our religion," as if religion can be one's ancestral property. Religion is never "mine" or "yours"—religion is that which sustains all of us.

Now this man ... has no idea of what he is doing. He is only disgracing his religion and making an exhibition of his stupidity and ignorance. His religion is not going to be saved like this. He is only showing how impotent his religion is. He is telling us simply that now they have nothing else to offer—with them there is nothing intelligent left to be said.[34]

The ashram sannyasins were shaken by this event. The painful history of how Socrates, Jesus, and Mansoor were disposed of and scores of other Buddhas tortured became fresh in their memories. Ma Yoga Laxmi, managing trustee of the Rajneesh Foundation, said in a press release:

Today, in Buddha Hall, the history of assassination, abuse and hostility which has been India's reaction to all its great mystics and seers repeated itself. These are the people who stoned Bud-

dha, tortured Mahavir and who now wish to silence Bhagwan. . . . These fanatics thought they could dispose of Bhagwan
in the same way that they disposed of Gandhi, but the divine
grace of existence decreed otherwise. Bhagwan will continue to
speak the truth, no matter how many attempts are made to prevent him from doing so.[35]

The accused, the would-be assassin, was charged, tried,
and acquitted.

Regardless of threats to Bhagwan's life and the negative
reactions of the press, priests, pundits, and politicians, the
ashram activities functioned normally. The energy-field
continued to grow. Security in and around the ashram was
tightened. Bhagwan's health remained very good. The remaining part of the year 1980 passed relatively calmly.

7. The
Silent Sage

THE YEAR 1981 will remain the most eventful year for the ashram. It began with one more disciple of Bhagwan attaining enlightenment. Thirty-three-year-old Swami Anand Vimalkirti, formerly Prince Welf of Hanover, reached enlightenment on the evening of January 9, 1981. He died and attained *Mahaparinirvana* (freedom from birth and death) on January 10, 1981. The story of this event, in brief, is as follows.

On January 5, while Vimalkirti was doing his daily "warm-up" exercises, he collapsed from a cerebral hemorrhage. He was kept alive in a Poona hospital for five days on respiratory machines. His mother, Princess Sophia, and his brother, Prince Georg, came from Germany to be with him.

Bhagwan paid his tribute to Vimalkirti in the morning discourse[1] in the following words:

Vimalkirti is blessed. He was one of those few of my chosen sannyasins who never wavered for a single moment, whose trust has been total the whole time he was here. He never asked a question, he never wrote a letter, he never brought any problem. His trust was such that he became by and by absolutely merged with me. He has one of the rarest hearts. That quality of the heart has disappeared from the world. He is really a prince, really royal, really aristocratic! Aristocracy has nothing to do with birth, it has something to do with the quality of the heart. And I experienced him as one of the rarest, most beautiful souls on the earth.[2]

Bhagwan wanted Vimalkirti to be kept on the respiratory machines for at least seven days, because, as Bhagwan explained:

He was just on the edge—a little push and he would become part of the beyond. . . . Hence I wanted him to hang around a little more. Last night he managed: he crossed the boundary from doing to non-doing. . . . "

Bhagwan also explained that because of his meditative quality Vimalkirti succeeded in disidentifying from his body and thus attaining consciousness beyond the body. Bhagwan continued:

You cannot get identified with such a body: the kidneys not functioning, the breathing not functioning, the heart not functioning, the brain totally damaged. How can you get identified with such a body? Impossible. Just a little alertness and you will become separate—and that much alertness he had, that much he had grown. So he immediately became aware that, "I am not the body, I am not the mind, I am not the heart either." And when you pass beyond these three, the fourth, *turiya,* is attained, and that is your real nature. Once it is attained it is never lost.

Bhagwan declared:

He will not need to come back again into a body; he is going awakened, he is going in the state of Buddhahood. . . . Get ready, rejoice, dance—dance to abandon! Let him go like a prince. He *was* a prince. Everyone of my sannyasins is a prince. I don't believe in beggars, I believe only in emperors![3]

Bhagwan expressed his happiness in the following words:

I am happy with him . . . and many of you are getting ready in the same way. I am really happy with my people! I don't think there has ever been a Master who had so many beautiful disciples. Jesus was very poor in that sense—not a single disciple became enlightened. Buddha was the richest in the past, but I am determined to defeat Gautam the Buddha.[4]

All members of Vimalkirti's family, including his wife, Ma Prem Turiya (formerly Princess Wibke of Hanover, also a sannyasin), daughter, Ma Prem Tania (formerly Princess Tania of Hanover), his father, Prince Georg Wilhelm of Hanover, mother, and brother, joined thousands of sannyasins to carry his body to the cremation ground. While Vimalkirti's body was burning on the pyre, everyone danced and sang in celebration. Messages of condolence were received from Queen Elizabeth II of England, H. R. H. Prince Charles of England (Vimalkirti was the nephew of the Queen and a cousin to Prince Charles), Queen Fredericka of Greece, Mrs. Indira Gandhi, and many other prominent people.[5]

The spirit of celebration not only continued as ever in the ashram, but it began to spread to other parts of the world. The biggest celebration ever organized by disciples of Bhagwan outside Poona took place at London's prestigious Cafe Royal on March 14–15, 1981. It was called "The March Event" and was in response to growing British interest in Bhagwan and the activities of Shree Rajneesh Ashram, Poona. Over a thousand people, including journalists and many other prominent people, participated in this two-day program of meditation and group therapy. Seven expert sannyasin group leaders conducted the program.

Following the overwhelming success of the "March Event," plans got underway to hold similar types of celebrations in San Francisco, Sidney, Berlin, and Munich. This spreading out of Bhagwan's message and work through his sannyasins was precisely as Bhagwan himself had envisioned it. He had said before that the time had come to extend his "Buddhafield"—the energy-field created by the Enlightened Master—all over the world. Since he himself

attained enlightenment he left no stone unturned to make
the fact of enlightenment available to as many people as
possible, which is clearly evident from the story of his life
and work up till now. He has declared:

I will be sending you to the four corners of the earth. You will be
my ambassadors at large, you will function for me. I will see
through your eyes, and I will speak through your tongues, and I
will touch people through your hands, and I will love through
your love.[6]

Bhagwan's message of love came through once again on
the twenty-eighth anniversary of his enlightenment—March
21, 1981. "My message for those who are thirsty for godli-
ness is this: this is a tavern and not a temple," said Bhagwan. He explained in the morning discourse that his
religion has no name because love has no name:

Love is neither Christian, nor Hindu, nor Muslim, nor Jain, nor
Buddhist. And if love has no name, how can religion—which is
the ultimate in love—have a name? Don't ask for a name; the
drunk have no religion, they have only drunkenness, only bliss.

And, in reference to the ashram and its organization, he
added:

Even a tavern needs a little organization. Someone has to see
that the thirsty are not left thirsty, and that the non-thirsty are not
allowed to trespass.[7]

No one had the slightest idea that the Master was just
about ready to reveal a new dimension of his work, and
that from now on he was going to be available to only
those who were ready to drink without the help of his
words—in silence. For many years Bhagwan had been telling his disciples that truth could never be expressed
through words. He said repeatedly that the disciple could
enter into communion with the Master only through profound silence:

Words are too profane, too inadequate, too limited. Only an empty space, utterly silence, can represent the being of the Buddha. Because you cannot understand silence, it has to be translated into language—otherwise there is no need.[8]

He had said in 1978:

At the highest peak of understanding, words are almost meaningless. Soon I hope the day will come when you will be able to understand my silence. Then I can stop using words.[9]

We have also seen in the previous chapter the meaning and significance of silence explained by Bhagwan when he was ill for ten days in June, 1979.

The evening darshan of March 23, 1981, turned out to be of immense significance—it was Bhagwan's last darshan to disciples and visitors. The discourse the next morning also turned out to be his last. It so happened that on the twenty-fourth several cases of chicken pox were spotted in the ashram,[10] and extra precautions were taken and the persons affected by the disease were immediately quarantined. Evening darshans were cancelled, and instead of morning discourse, silent music meditation began in Buddha Hall from the twenty-fifth on.

At the last darshan of March 23, Bhagwan talked about the origin of words and language. He mentioned in particular the classic statement made in the Bible that, "In the beginning was the Word, and the Word was with God and the Word was God." Bhagwan responded to this statement:

I say categorically no! In the beginning was silence and also in the end is silence. Silence is the stuff the universe is made of. And I can say it authentically because if one goes within oneself, one comes to the beginning of everything, because you contain both the beginning and the end.[11]

Despite the cases of chicken pox, the canceling of the darshans, and absence of early morning discourses of the

Master, the ashram activities continued smoothly. Everyone expected Bhagwan to come out on April 11, when the next meditation camp was to begin and Bhagwan was to start the lecture series in English. However, on April 10, Ma Anand Sheela, one of the trustees of Rajneesh Foundation, called a meeting of all department heads of the ashram and announced over a glass of wine that Bhagwan was entering into a new and ultimate state of his work—he was entering into silence. She was among the first ones to hear of Bhagwan's decision. Sheela was shocked to hear the news from Bhagwan. She said:

But Bhagwan said there was no need to be shocked, he said we should all be happy, celebrate. And he asked me to convey it to the others with the same feeling of joy which he felt.

In the ashram, the news spread like wildfire. It came as a genuine surprise to many. But within a few hours everyone in the ashram was singing and dancing. The disciples soon realized that the time had come for them to go into a deeper level and have a real communion with the Master.

In a historical declaration, the Rajneesh Foundation announced that Bhagwan Shree Rajneesh had begun the ultimate stage of his work. Also, it was announced that Bhagwan had stopped giving morning discourses in English and Hindi. From May 1, 1981, on Bhagwan would speak only through silence, which he had described as "the language of existence." Instead of verbal communication there would be a *satsang*, a silent heart-to-heart communion, it was announced. It was stated further that a certain number of disciples were ready to receive Bhagwan in silence; hence, he would make himself available only to them. The disciples were now able to enter into a silent spiritual communion with the Master, on a deeper and more profound level. Satsang would take place every morning in Buddha Hall from eight-thirty to nine-thirty.

A new phase had also started for the evening darshan at

the ashram, the announcement said. Bhagwan himself would no longer be physically present. Ma Yoga Laxmi, Swami Ananda Teertha, and I (when Laxmi was away) were declared to be the mediums for this work. When the declaration was made, Laxmi was out of town for Foundation work, hence evening darshans for Indian friends, sannyas, blessings, and energy darshans were given by me, while for Western friends, sannyas, blessings, and energy were given by Teertha.[12]

After having astounded the public with his revolutionary and original views on almost every possible subject under the sun, Bhagwan's decision to enter into silence produced reactions all around the world that ranged from genuine surprise to complete disbelief and cynicism. Nevertheless, the fact remained that Bhagwan had been waiting for this moment. He had been preparing disciples for this ultimate phase of his work; he had been preparing them for independence. His decision showed clearly that the disciples had become receptive enough for this new dimension, so there was a feeling of joy and of mystery among them. Although there was a deep feeling that they would miss his voice and his insights which used to make their day flow, there was no alarm. In fact, there was a feeling of gratitude among the disciples, because Bhagwan had found them worthy enough to share the last phase of silence.

The new phase provided everyone with the opportunity to experience Bhagwan's energy independently from his physical presence in the evening darshan, and also without the aid of his communication through words in the discourses. He withdrew even further from his disciples, as far as this outer part of his being was concerned, and entered into a deeper intimacy with them. He had pointed out to them long before that:

The day you are able to see this chair empty, this body empty, this being empty, you will have seen me; you will have contacted me. That is the real moment when the disciple meets the Master. It is a dissolution, a disappearance . . . the dewdrop slipping into the ocean, or, the ocean slipping into the dewdrop. It is the same! —the Master disappearing into the disciple and the disciple disappearing into the Master. And then there prevails profound silence. It is not a dialogue.[13]

On May 1, 1981, Bhagwan gave his first *satsang* as a "silent sage" to an audience of over six thousand disciples and visitors in Buddha Hall. This was his first appearance since he stopped giving the daily discourse on March 24, 1981. The satsang lasted for one hour—it was a wordless, heart-to-heart communion between the Master and his devotees. The satsang began with the chanting of a mantra which was used once before by the commune of *bhikkhus* (disciples) who gathered around Gautam Buddha twenty-five hundred years ago: *"Buddham sharanam gachchami, Sangham sharanam gachchami, Dhammam sharanam gachchami . . ."* ("I go to the feet of the Awakened One, I go to the feet of the commune of the Awakened One, I go to the feet of the ultimate truth of the Awakened One.") After the mantra was chanted, soft, meditative music was played, interspersed with periods of silence. In between, passages from the *Isha Upanishad* and Khalil Gibran's *The Prophet* were read. At the end, the mantra was repeated and Bhagwan left the hall.

The satsang continued to take place every morning. Bhagwan would sit in silence with his sannyasins for one hour. Vivek would accompany him on the podium and sit at his feet. Bhagwan had explained the meaning and purpose of satsang:

Being near a Master who has become one with the truth. The Master is not going to do anything, he is simply there available. If you are open he will flow into you.

Being silent, hearing silence, doing nothing and being interior, deeper than all expression, that is satsang. One simply sits with the Master, feeling his presence, becoming part of his energy-field, breathing with him, pulsating with him. Slowly, slowly, the ego dissolves of its own accord, just as the sun rises and the snow starts melting. [14]

Withdrawing even further from activities, Bhagwan's silence, in another way, evidently manifests his being in the state of the third guna—sattva. He had already passed through the first two gunas—tamas, and rajas. Describing the nature of sattva guna, Bhagwan says that:

As the rajas guna subsides and the effects of the sattva guna begin to appear, all actions dissolve into silence. In the state of tamas, all actions cease, but that ceasing is like that of one going to sleep. In the sattvic state also all actions dissolve into silence, but that dissolution is into total awareness.

The principles or qualities of inactivity (tamas) and serenity (sattva) have one thing in common—they both end in silence, explains Bhagwan. He adds, however, that the

Form of silence arising out of the principle of inactivity will be that of sleep, whereas the form of silence arising from the principle of serenity will be that of silent awareness. [15]

Bhagwan's silence, however, had an added dimension— the dimension of music. Explaining the relation between music and silence, Bhagwan says:

Music in a sense is absolutely silent. Sounds are there, but those sounds only make the silence deeper, they help the silence. . . . Noise is just sound which does not lead you to silence. Music is sound that becomes a door to silence.

Bhagwan explains further:

The being of a Master is the being of music, poetry, song. But they all lead to silence, and truth can only be conveyed in silence. [16]

While the disciples experienced the loving and blissful company of their Master in this deep, new dimension, the world outside grew more and more hostile and violent toward Bhagwan, the disciples, and the ashram. There was an alarming increase in the number of threatening letters and telephone calls received at the ashram. They included threats against the life of Bhagwan as well as against the lives of individual disciples. For example, an offer of a quarter of a million pounds was made to a man in Sri Lanka for his help in killing Bhagwan. A letter received on May 3 by a sannyasin at the ashram revealed this information. It read, "A guy asked me to help him kill Bhagwan. . . . He said he was going to offer me a quarter of a million pounds if I helped him. He has given me two weeks to consider. . . . " The writer of the letter also revealed that the offer was made by a "muni"—maybe a Jain *muni* (Jain monk)—and added in the letter: "They hate Bhagwan."[17]

The news release issued by the Rajneesh Foundation press office on May 10 brought this alarming situation to the attention of the press. The news release mentioned, among other things, that a threat had come from a group called "Roman Catholics of Bombay and Poona," who warned that they would hurt Bhagwan and bomb the ashram. A message was received that implied that a secret organization was to launch a campaign of violence against the ashram. I was also singled out for threats of violence, following the appearance of a newspaper article I wrote explaining the teachings of Bhagwan.

The news release quoted one of the Foundation's officials as saying:

These threats are an admission of defeat by people who cannot answer Bhagwan in any other way. For example, these so-called Christians who are threatening us are simply demonstrating the bankruptcy of their Christian ideals.

They cannot argue with Bhagwan on his own terms, so they have to resort to threats of murder and violence, they do not belong to Jesus Christ at all—in fact, if Jesus were alive today they would help to crucify him. The same is true of the Hindu and Jain fanatics who also threaten us. They are all afraid of Bhagwan because they know he is revealing the truth.[18]

And the threats began to be carried out. A fire occurred at Rajneeshdham, Jadhavwadi Fort, Saswad, in the early morning hours of May 27. Twenty-four hours later, on May 28, arson destroyed a Rajneesh Foundation book storage warehouse located near Poona. Several explosions were heard in rapid succession and fire spread quickly through the stacked books. The blaze started at around three o'clock in the morning. At about the same time an explosive device detonated at the Foundation's medical center. Fortunately, no one was hurt.

In spite of the attacks, the morning satsang with Bhagwan took place as usual in Buddha Hall. Before satsang began, a gathering of over three thousand disciples and visitors raised their arms in a demonstration of protest and condemnation against the outrages. Ma Prem Arup, one of the Foundation officials, issued a statement in which she said:

Our only concern is for Bhagwan. But whatever the risk, what he is offering to humanity will continue to be offered. His message to the world is so important that it cannot be stopped by fanatics.[19]

The disciples had taken the events of arson and hostility with calmness and with increasing trust and devotion toward their Master. They remained near him in silence, in prayer, in deep love, and surrender. The work and activities of the ashram continued without interruption. But Bhagwan's health again began to fail and it was clear that he would have to go to the West for medical treatment. Consequently, Bhagwan's last satsang took place on the morning of June 1, 1981. He bid goodbye to his beloved disciples the same afternoon and left Poona as quietly as he had arrived seven years earlier.

A group of sannyasins accompanied Bhagwan on the journey to America aboard a Pan Am jet. He was brought to the Chidvilas Rajneesh Meditation Center, Montclair, New Jersey, where all the necessary arrangements were made for his medical care and rest.

Bhagwan was asked occasionally whether or not he would ever leave India, and every time his answer was that he would not. He explained the reasons for his not leaving India in a discourse on August 30, 1978.

It is difficult for me to leave India. India has something tremendously valuable. It has the longest, deepest search for truth. Many Buddhas have walked on this land, under these trees; the very earth has become sacred. To be here is totally different than to be anywhere else. And what I am trying to bring to you is more easily possible here than anywhere else.

India has fallen from its peaks. It is no more its past glory. It is one of the ugliest spots now on the earth, but still, because a Gautam Buddha walked, and a Mahavira and a Krishna, and millions of others . . .

No other country can claim this. Jesus is very alone in Jerusalem; Mohammed is very very alone in the Arabian countries; Lao Tzu has had a very small company—Chuang Tzu and a few others. They tried hard to create something. But India has the longest spiritual vibe. At least for five thousand years the search has been deepening.

And still the waters are flowing.

This India that you see in the newspapers, this India I have left already. The India that you know, I have left already. Have you ever seen me going out of the gate? I live in my room. Whether this room is here or anywhere else, I will live in the room. It will be the same. I have left this India already. I am not concerned with this India that you come to know through radio, television, newspapers—the India of the politicians, of the hypocrites, of the masochistic mahatmas. I have left it already.

But I cannot leave. There is a hidden India, too, an esoteric India too, where Buddhas are still alive, where you can contact Mahavira more easily than anywhere else, where the whole tradition of the awakened ones is like an undercurrent. I can't leave that. For me, there is no problem—I can leave; I will be the same anywhere—but for you it will not be the same.[20]

But Bhagwan did leave India. Why? Perhaps part of the answer was revealed just one month before Bhagwan stopped speaking in public. One question that was often asked concerned the fate of the movement that has grown around Bhagwan after he leaves his body. To this question, he gave an elaborate and clear reply which turned out to be his last English discourse. Bhagwan said:

I am living my moment. I don't care a bit about what happens later on. It may look very irresponsible to you because my criterion of responsibility is diametrically opposite to people's idea of so-called responsibility. I am responsible to the moment, to existence—and responsible not in the sense of being dutiful to it, responsible in the sense that I respond totally, spontaneously. Whatsoever the situation is, I am utterly in tune with it. While I am alive I am alive, when I am dead I will be dead. I don't see any question at all.

The moment I die, the whole world dies for me; then whatsoever happens, happens. I have not taken on the whole responsibility for existence. Who can take it? But there have been people who have tried it and they have all utterly failed.

I am not controlling anybody—I am not a politician. I am not interested at all that anybody should be controlled by me today or tomorrow.

And when I am not there, what can I do? Fools are fools. Whether they worship me or somebody else will not make much difference. If they want to worship they will worship.

Every institution is bound to be dead, only a man is alive. No institution is ever alive. How can an institution be alive? By its very nature it is going to be dead.

As far as I am concerned, I am not at all interested in the next moment. Even if this sentence remains incomplete, I will not make any effort to complete it. I will not even put a full point to it. I have no desire to dominate, but I cannot go on saying to people, "Don't worship me," because that is the way to create worship.

People always misunderstand. While the Master is alive they will not come to him because while the Master is alive, they cannot be allowed to misunderstand. They will come to him only when he is no longer there, because a dead Master can be controlled, manipulated.

First, I am a man who is consistently inconsistent. It will not be possible to make a dogma out of my words; anybody trying to make a creed or dogma out of my words will go nuts! You can make a dogma out of Mahavira—he is a very consistent man, very logical. You can make a philosophy out of Buddha—he is very mathematical. You can make a philosophy out of Krishnamurti—for fifty years he has been simply repeating the same thing again and again; you cannot find a single inconsistency in him.

It is impossible with me: I live in the moment and whatsoever I am saying right now is true only for this moment. I have no reference with my past and I don't think of the future at all. So my statements are atomic; they are not part of a system. And you can make a dead institution only when a philosophy is very systematic, when there are no more flaws, when no fault can be found, when all doubts are solved, all questions dissolved and you are given a ready-made answer to everything in life.

I am so inconsistent that it is impossible to create a dead institution around me because a dead institution will need the infrastructure of a dead philosophy. I am not teaching you any doctrine, I am not giving you any principles; on the contrary, I am trying to take away all the philosophies that you have carried all along. I am destroying your ideologies, creeds, cults, dogmas, and I am not replacing them with anything else. My process is of pure deconditioning. I am not trying to recondition you. I leave you open.

I am simply sharing my vision, my joy. I am enjoying it, and whosoever wants to enjoy it with me is welcome. Naturally, when I am gone there may be a few fools who will try to figure it out, to make a system, although I am making it almost impossible.

These people who are wondering what will happen are the same people who will create a dead institution. My people cannot create a dead institution—it is impossible. Those who have been in communion with me will have learnt one thing absolutely, categorically: that life cannot be confined into institutions; the moment you try to confine it into institutions you destroy it. So while I am alive they will celebrate. When I am gone they will still celebrate. They will celebrate my life, they will celebrate my death; and they will remain alive.

I am preparing my people to live joyously, ecstatically, so when I am not here, it won't make any difference to them. They will still live in the same way and maybe my death will bring them more intensity.

I am not leaving anything to anybody. I have declared myself Bhagwan. Why should I leave it to anybody? I know I am the Blessed One, and only I can know. How can anybody else know it? And I am trying to seduce my people into understanding this immensity: that they are also the Blessed Ones. It is impossible to deify me—I have already done it! What else is there left for you? I don't depend on anybody.[21]

It is clear that Bhagwan is not confined to any boundaries, including the boundaries of a particular nation or state. He is concerned with the whole humanity. He can be just as available for inspiration and blessings in America, or anywhere else in the world, as he was in India.

It has been widely reported in the American media that a new location of about 64,000 acres has been bought by the Rajneesh Foundation International near Antelope, Oregon. This may become the place for the realization of Bhagwan's vision:

The new commune will be on a big scale: . . . sannyasins living together as one body, one being. Nobody will possess anything: everybody will use; everybody will enjoy. Everybody is going to live as comfortably, as richly as we can manage, but nobody will possess anything. Not only will things not be possessed, but persons will also not be possessed in the new commune. If you love a woman, live with her—out of sheer love, out of sheer joy—but don't become her husband. You can't. Don't become a wife. To become a wife or a husband is ugly because it brings ownership, and then the other is reduced to property.

The new commune is going to be nonpossessive, full of love—living in love but with no possessiveness at all; sharing all kinds of joys, making a pool of all the joys. . . .

In my commune, Buddha is going to laugh and dance, Christ

is going to laugh and dance. Poor fellows, nobody has allowed them that up to now! Have compassion on them: let them dance and sing and play.

My new commune is going to transform work into playfulness. It is going to transform life into love and laughter. Remember the motto again: to hallow the earth; to make everything sacred; to transform the ordinary, mundane things into extraordinary, spiritual things. The whole life has to be your temple. Work has to be your worship. Love has to be your prayer.

This very body, the Buddha; this very earth, the lotus paradise.[22]

Epilogue

In the last decade, many countercultural, personal growth, and neo-Christian movements (mainly embracing Eastern mysticism) have emerged in the West. They have also been referred to as the "metaphysical movement." It has been suggested[1] that the involvement of Western people in countercultural type groups is basically a transient phenomenon, attributable to the youthfulness of the individuals involved and their tendency toward adolescent exploration. Yet another reason given for such involvement is that the dominant cultural ethic has failed to provide youth with collective and viable cultural alternatives, while the alternative solutions proposed by the counterculture have greatly attracted them.

It has also been suggested that the individuals who pursue altered states of consciousness like the ones experienced in mystical groups are people most alienated from society[2] and who are experiencing considerable frustration in their personal and social lives. It has been pointed out by the observers, however, that the individuals involved in these new movements are engaged in a creative effort at resolving "the duplication of consciousness." In other words, they are attempting to bring about a resolution between the identity assigned by society and/or acquired by their objective understanding, and their self-perceived subjective identity. It has been stressed further that at a time when there is widespread feeling of meaninglessness in Western society, and when the traditional religious systems have failed to provide any psychological and spiritual solution to the existing problems, the emergence of these new groups represents a significant force for social change.

Bhagwan's observation and assessment of the West and its problems carries much deeper insight. He does not stop at diagnosing the problem—he also provides a vision to lift not only the West, but the entire world, to a much higher level of existence. His observation of the current situation is that "either the West will commit suicide through atomic war for which it is preparing, or there will be a spiritual awakening ... the greatest spiritual awakening that has ever happened in the history of man."[3]

Bhagwan has taken a critical look at the existentialist philosophy that has represented Western thought so dominantly in the last hundred or so years. In reference to Sartre, for example, Bhagwan says that he was not true to his philosophy, for he merely talked about things like courage, sincerity, authenticity, and so forth, but did not translate them into his life. If life had to in fact be *that* full of misery, then one would either commit suicide or bring about transformation of his life—what is the point of continuing to remain miserable and keep rationalizing such existence? "It seems," says Bhagwan, "that this despair, anguish, meaninglessness, is also verbal, logical but not existential." Bhagwan expresses his view of existentialism in the following words:

It is my feeling that the existentialism of the West is not really existentialist; it is again a philosophy. To be existentialist means it must be a feeling, not a thinking. Sartre may be a great thinker— he is, but he has not felt the thing, he has not lived it. If you live in despair, you are bound to come to a point where something has to be done, radically done, immediately done, a transformation becomes urgent, becomes your only concern.[4]

Illustrating from the life story of Buddha, Bhagwan distinguishes between the Eastern and the Western views of reality and thus focuses sharply upon the element missing in the existentialists. Narrating the story of Buddha, he says:

He comes to see an old man, he realizes that youth is just a passing phase, a momentary phenomenon; a wave in the ocean rising and falling, nothing of permanence in it, nothing of the eternal in it; just like a dream, a bubble ready to burst any moment. Then he sees a dead man being carried. In the West the story would have stopped there: the old man, the dead man. But in the Indian story, after the dead man he sees a sannyasin—that is the door. And then he asks his driver, "Who is this man, and why is he in ochre robes? What has happened to him? What type of man is he?" The driver says, "This man has also realized that life leads to death and he is in search of a life which is deathless."

This was the milieu: life does not end with death. Buddha's story shows that after seeing death, when life feels meaningless, suddenly a new dimension arises, a new vision—sannyas: the effort to penetrate into the deeper mystery of life, to penetrate deeper into the visible to reach the invisible, to penetrate matter so deeply that matter disappears and you come to the basic reality, the reality of spiritual energy, the Brahma. With Sartre, Camus, Heidegger, the story ends with the dead man. The sannyasin is missing, that is the missing link.[5]

Bhagwan has shown the link, he has provided the link, "sannyas" (or neo-sannyas) is his gift that has fulfilled the need—especially for the West. In Bhagwan's vision now a sannyasin has to appear in the West: one who is rooted in the West, who has experienced the meaninglessness, the frustration, the utter disappointment brought by the materialist philosophy. "My whole interest," declares Bhagwan,

is to make as many Western people sannyasins as possible and send them back home. Many Sartres are waiting there. They have seen the death. They are waiting to see the ochre robe, and with the ochre robe, the ecstasy that follows.[6]

One may ask: How did Bhagwan read the Western mind? How did he feel their pulse? In order to discover the answer to these questions, we shall have to probe a little deeper into the nature and dimension of the contact that occurred between Bhagwan and the seekers from the West. It is quite clear that apart from his voracious reading (about one hundred books per week, according to Bhagwan's librarian) and thus being greatly informed about the world he is living in, his direct contact with thousands of people from the West made it possible for him to study Westerners, the Western mind, very closely and intimately. Hence, this is not just a contact between a seeker and a seer, or between a master and a disciple. Far more than that, it is a meeting, a union between the East and the West.

Although the growing interest in Eastern mysticism in the West and the revitalization of mysticism in the East itself have contributed to the "evolution of consciousness," the new spiritual or orange explosion that has happened recently in the West has given birth to a new consciousness that is neither spiritual nor material but is a synthesis of both. Bhagwan is the midwife of this new birth. He has become the strong link, a bridge in bringing about union between East and West. The seekers in search of someone who could unite the whole of humanity, someone who could assimilate various spiritual systems and coordinate various religious traditions without denying this world and the worldly life, found in Bhagwan the one who could do it—who was in fact doing it. "I am . . . bringing you a synthesis of East and West," he announced, "of science and religion, of intellect and intuition, of the male mind and the female mind, of the head and heart, of the right and the left. I am also trying in every possible way to create a great harmony, because only that harmony can save."[7]

In order to resolve conflicts between different religions, other individuals in history have tried before to create one religion. But the problem is not of having *a* religion or following *one* religion. The quest of the West concerns finding someone, an enlightened person, a living source, who could help individuals contact their own religious consciousness, who manifests a state of integrated religious consciousness. The therapy groups and the therapists trained under Bhagwan's guidance became a form of halfway point for the seekers from the West. The therapies and the therapists brought them closer to Bhagwan, and thus gave them an opportunity to see, touch, and feel what enlightenment was like, what it meant to be religious without necessarily following a particular religion. For the first time since Jesus, the West became aware and assured of the presence of Jesus.

Many masters, including Gurdjieff, have worked before Bhagwan toward coordinating different spiritual systems. They also attracted seekers from diverse paths to come together and work in love and harmony. But Gurdjieff, for example, did not succeed; his efforts did not come to fruition. His school disintegrated because it was so difficult to coordinate different systems of spirituality and create a cohesive group. Gurdjieff himself was a Buddha, but the time was not ripe for him to give concrete shape to his vision. This can be seen from what has become of Gurdjieff's group in the last fifty or so years. Gurdjieff himself had felt the incompleteness of his work.

For Bhagwan, the work already done by Gurdjieff and other masters proved very useful. It provided him with the background, made the soil ready. Most of those who came to Bhagwan from the West already had a psyche structure that could receive him. They were prepared, and they were ready to overcome the weaknesses that existed in them due to lack of guidance from a living master, one who not only understood their minds, but also knew how to work with them toward creating an integrated vision of life.

Bhagwan's study of the human mind and psyche has made him a forerunner in a field he calls "the third psychology" or "the psychology of Buddhas." Freud, Jung, Adler, and other psychologists gave birth to the first type of psychology, the psychology of the pathological mind. Maslow, Fromm, Janov, and others concentrated more on the growth of a healthy mind. Their approach was "holistic" and they gave birth to the second type of psychology, humanistic psychology. The third type of psychology, says Bhagwan, never existed before. Buddhas—who were beyond the pathological and the healthy mind, who were just "no-mind"—lived before, but none of them ever tried to make a scientific study of the awakened mind, except, as Bhagwan points out, Gurdjieff.

Gurdjieff was the first man in the whole history of humanity who tried. Gurdjieff is rare in this sense because he was a pioneer into the third possibility . . .

But P. D. Ouspensky, upon whom Gurdjieff depended for communicating his insights in a scientific way, left him in the middle. Bhagwan adds:

Gurdjieff tried and tried. He tried to find somebody else. He worked with many people but he could not find one of the caliber of Ouspensky. Ouspensky's growth stopped and Gurdjieff's work for the third psychology stopped.[8]

In view of the difficulties faced by Gurdjieff, Bhagwan took upon himself a double role. He has described the nature of his work in creating the third psychology:

I am again trying to work in the third dimension and I have not taken the risk that Gurdjieff took. I am not depending on anybody. I am Gurdjieff plus Ouspensky. It is hard work to live in two different dimensions. It is very hard, but anyway, it is good. Because nobody can betray me and stop my work—nobody. So I am continuously moving, in the world of no-mind and in the world of books and analysis. . . . I have been working continuously on both levels; there is every possibility that the effort can succeed.[9]

Thus Bhagwan has been studying and experimenting with Eastern and Western psyches but his work on the

Western psyche has been specially significant. The extroverted, earthly, hedonistic, science-oriented psyche; The psyche of those who are concerned with "how to do," with methods and systems—all these characteristics of the Western psyche are very familiar to him. He has observed keenly the various manifestations of the Western psyche and has in his own way seen the possibilities of working on it.

Yet another dimension of Bhagwan's contact with the West can be seen through a historical perspective. The new generation in the West, that is, the generation that witnessed enormous affluence on the one hand and the incredible death and destruction in Vietnam on the other, has been searching for new meaning in their lives. They have been searching for a new answer, a new reality—though certainly not of the utopian type. They want to learn how to live in total acceptance, in the here and now, with authenticity. Many from this new generation who were identified in general as "hippies" or "flower children" had a sense of direction, but they did not have the needed guidance. Their search brought them to the East. *They* were the first ones to come in touch with Bhagwan, not the academics, the sophisticated, the highbrows. Only the wanderers came in that early contact. Only the rebels, revolutionaries, radicals, all those who were searching for an alternative to their conditioned way of living, came to Bhagwan.

So these "mad people," whom Bhagwan calls "my people," were the first ones to approach him, to fall in love with him. They were accepted and unconditionally loved by him, without exception. They received some initial energy from Bhagwan and then went back to their own countries and began spreading the news about Bhagwan. They assured others like themselves that there was someone who could bring them out of their misery, pain, and frustration. On one hand, these early Westerners functioned to spread Bhagwan's message to others, and on the other, they functioned to bring information, feedback to Bhagwan. They provided him with firsthand understanding of what was occurring in the social as well as psychological realms of the West. It was only subsequent to this initial work done by the "hippies," "flower children," and "dropouts," that more educated, refined, and sophisticated people started to be drawn to Bhagwan. It took several years for the intellectuals, the academics, the rationalists to realize that there was someone who, instead of answering their questions, was able to bring about such a radical change in their perspective that the very questions dropped away or evaporated, and they felt deeply relaxed, almost ecstatic.

The point is that the mystic and the member of the intelligentsia constitute two ends of a continuum—the middle contains the raw, the rebel, the dropout. Bhagwan's mystic energy first touched this middle category. This middle is the bridge; these people in the middle paved the way because the refined, the intellectual would not listen to the mystic who is always absurd, nonrational, inconsistent, and beyond logic. Thus only the raw young energy of those who were ready to be vulnerable and receptive, those who carried a particular type of innocence, became the bridge for Bhagwan in reaching the established, the old guards.

Thus the movement around Bhagwan did not begin accidentally; rather, it was the product of a thorough, systematic, and rather rhythmic process that has had a long, continuous growth. His vision of making Buddhahood available to all required a process far deeper and more subtle, a process that has already given birth to a new man. During his years in Poona the work and the movement grew considerably. People initiated and helped by him are in large enough numbers to carry on the process even deeper and wider in the West.

How, one may ask, is the East-West contact through Bhagwan and the movement around him different from past meetings of East and West? The most significant differ-ence is that in the past, especially in the nineteenth century (and even in this century), people either came to India with or looked at India through the dichotomous view of "East is East and West is West." This view was based more or less on prejudice and on ignorance of the commonalities that exist beneath the social and cultural patterns of the separate societies of East and West. Similarly, those who went from India to the West had no understanding of it. They just wanted to take the spiritual message from India to the West, while maintaining the overly generalized and dichotomized opinion that the West was very different from the East—that West was all materialistic and the East was all spiritualistic.

Bhagwan has proved himself to be a realist; he does not have a divided view. In fact, he does not have a divided view about anything, he accepts everything: soul and body, matter and spirit, love and meditation, East and West. He sees the whole of humanity in the same boat. He knows the West as well as he knows the East. He knows the world better than Mahavir, Buddha, Jesus, Mohammed, or any other spiritual leader ever did before. He is placed in a time when he can see and respond to the condition of the world through a greater and more highly sophisticated informa-tion system. His contribution to the growth of human con-sciousness is not local—it is global.

Finally, Sri Aurobindo once wrote to his biographer disci-ple, "Neither you nor anyone else knows anything at all of my life, it has not been on the surface for men to see."[10] Bhagwan has expressed a similar view, and I feel little hesi-tation in admitting that in spite of writing this story, I know nothing about Bhagwan, simply because he is not just a person, he is a phenomenon.

Many from the East and the West have tried to experi-ence Bhagwan, to be receptive to his teachings and inter-pret his work to others. Given below are two views about

Bhagwan that fairly sum up these attempts. First, Bernard Levin, of the *Times* in London, who wrote about his experience after spending some time in Poona ashram:

... But if he is God, he is a very undeified one, and certainly in his discourses there is no hint even of "Who say ye that I am?" only a powerful sense that he is a conduit along which the vital force of the universe flows. (One of the ashram-dwellers, when I asked the same question—What do you regard Rajneesh as?—put it impressively in two words: "a reminder.") ...

I came away impressed, moved, fascinated by my experience of this man (or God, or conduit, or reminder) and the people ... around him.[11]

M. V. Kamath, the editor of *The Illustrated Weekly of India,* a widely circulated and respected English weekly in India, made the following remarks:

... There has been no other man like this before. One may criticize Rajneesh, but it is impossible to ignore him. ... Like Whitman, Rajneesh is an iconoclast, a maverick, a hater of cant, superstition, snobbery and holier-than-thou'ism and a lover of the good things of life. He will make a most remarkable statement of purpose and philosophy and illustrate it with the most outrageous joke or story picked straight from *Playboy* or *Penthouse.* There is no way one can compartmentalise this man. It would almost seem that he is not one man but many men.

... Rajneesh is Moses, Walt Whitman, Buddha, Jesus Christ and Ramana Maharshi all rolled into one. Every individual has a little of them but Rajneesh seems to have more of them than the rest of us.

... It is ridiculous to try to define this man. He challenges definition. His technique is to put everything upside down on its head, so to speak, and make you look at the world from that vantage point. He is a disturbing man because he makes you question the validity of all your principles. ...

... Shakespeare may have had him in mind when he said: *Take him for all in all, I shall not look upon his like again.* Take him all in all or not at all, Rajneesh leaves no choices.[12]

Appendix A: Meditations

Dynamic Meditation

This technique can be done in a group or alone, but the energy will be more potent if it is done with others. The meditator can use a blindfold, and should have an empty stomach and wear a minimum of clothing.

First Stage: 10 minutes. Deep, fast, chaotic breathing through the nose. Be the breathing, forgetting the body and the mind, and let the body move as it needs to.

Second Stage: 10 minutes. Catharsis. Let go, be mad. Scream, cry, jump, shake, dance, laugh. Cooperate with the energy and with anything that happens, as totally as possible.

Third Stage: 10 minutes. With raised arms, jump up and down shouting hoo! hoo! hoo! so that the sound hammers deep into the sex center. Give all you have, exhaust yourself in reaching a crescendo.

Fourth Stage: 15 minutes. Stop. Freeze where you are, in whatever position you find yourself in. Witness the energy in silence within.

Fifth Stage. 15 minutes. Dance, sing, rejoice in celebration and thanksgiving.

For those who are unable to make noise where they are meditating, an alternative method is to keep all the sounds within,

---

* Material in Appendix A is adapted from *My People: A Community to Provoke God* (Poona: Rajneesh Foundation, 1978), pp. 43–51).

rather than throwing them out. For those who enter into it fully, this form of the meditation can go very deep. In the second stage allow the body to explode into a soundless catharsis in which the purging, the release, is done entirely through body movements. In the third stage hammer the sound hoo! hoo! deep inside. In the fifth stage, dance.

Kundalini Meditation

This meditation moves very potent energies within the meditator. Just as it is good to do the Dynamic at sunrise, this beautiful "sister" meditation should be done at sunset. Each of the four stages lasts 15 minutes.

First Stage: Be loose and let your whole body shake, feeling the energies moving up from your feet. Let go everywhere and become the shaking and shivering. Your eyes may be open or closed.

Second Stage: Dance . . . any way you feel, and let the whole body move as it wishes.

Third Stage: Be still, standing or sitting . . . witnessing.

Fourth Stage: Lie down . . . be still.

Mandala Meditation

Each stage of this powerful and energetic meditation lasts 15 minutes.

First Stage: With eyes open run on the spot, bringing your knees up as high as possible. Let your breathing be deep and even. This will move the energy within.

Second Stage: Sit with closed eyes, mouth loose and open. Gently sway. This will bring your awakened energies to the naval center.

Third Stage: Lie back and rotate your open eyes in a clockwise direction. Sweep them fully round in the sockets as if you are following a vast clock, but as fast as possible. Your mouth should be relaxed and open, head perfectly still and the breathing soft and gentle. This will bring your centered energies to the third eye.

Fourth Stage: Close your eyes and be still.

Nataraj

Many meditation techniques use dancing, for *"when the dance is there, the dancer is not."* Nataraj is dance as a total meditation.

First Stage: 40 minutes. Dance as if possessed. Let your unconscious take over completely. Do not control your movements or be a witness, just be totally in the dance.

Second Stage: 20 minutes. Lie down immediately, silent and still. Allow the vibrations of the dance and the music to penetrate your most subtle layers.

Third Stage: 5 minutes. Dance in celebration and enjoy.

Devavani Meditation

Devavani means the divine voice which moves and speaks through the meditator, who becomes an empty vessel, a channel. In the New Testament it was termed glossolalia.

Four stages of 15 minutes each. Eyes closed throughout.

First Stage: Sit quietly, preferably to gentle music.

Second Stage: Start allowing words to form, at first with "la . . . la . . . la. . . " until unfamiliar yet seemingly wordlike sounds occur. The "words" need to come from the unfamiliar part of the brain used as a child before words were learnt. Do not cry or shout, laugh or scream. Just allow a gentle conversational intonation.

Third Stage: Standing up, continue to speak and allow your body to softly move in accord with the sound. If you relax and are loose, the subtle energies will move your body without your control.

Fourth Stage: Lie down and be silent and still.

Laughing Meditation

Every morning upon waking, before opening your eyes, stretch like a cat. Stretch every fiber of your body. After three or four minutes, with eyes still closed, begin to laugh. For five minutes just laugh. At first you will be doing it, but soon the sound of your attempt will cause genuine laughter. Lose yourself in laughter. It may take several days before it really happens, for we are so unaccustomed to the phenomenon, but before long it will be spontaneous and will change the whole nature of your day.

Gourishankar Meditation

Bhagwan has said that if breathing is done correctly in the first stage, the carbon dioxide formed in the bloodstream will make the meditator feel as high as if on Gourishankar (Mt. Everest). Four stages, 15 minutes each.

First Stage: Sit with eyes closed. Inhale deeply through the nose, filling the lungs. Hold the breath for as long as possible, then exhale gently through the mouth, keeping the lungs empty for as long as possible. Repeat this cycle.

Second Stage: Return to normal breathing and, allowing the gaze to be soft and gentle, look at a candle flame or flashing light. Keep the body still.

Third Stage: With eyes closed, stand up and let the body be loose and receptive. The subtle energies within will be felt to move the body outside your normal control. Allow this (Latihan) to happen. Don't *you* do the moving, let moving happen.

Fourth Stage: Lie down, silent and still.

The first three stages should be accompanied by a steady rhythmic beat, preferably combined with soothing background music. The beat should be seven times the normal heartbeat and, if possible, the flashing light should be a synchronized strobe.

Nadabrahma I

This is an old Tibetan technique that was originally done in the very early hours of the morning. It is suggested that it be done either at night before going to sleep or during the morning, when it should be followed by at least 15 minutes rest. It can be done alone, with others, or even at work. It should be done on an empty stomach, otherwise the inner sound cannot go very deep.

First Stage: 30 minutes at least. Sit in a relaxed position with eyes closed, lips together. Begin to hum, loudly enough to create a vibration throughout the entire body. It should be loud enough to be heard by others. You can alter pitch and inhale as you please and if the body moves, allow it, providing that the movements are smooth and slow.

Visualize your body as a hollow tube, an empty vessel, filled only with the vibrations of the humming. A point will come where the humming occurs by itself and you become the listener. The brain is activated and every fiber cleansed. (This technique is particularly useful in healing.)

Second Stage: Move the hands, palms up, in a circular outward motion. The right hand moves to the right, the left to the left. Make these circles large, moving as slowly as possible. At times the hands will appear not to be moving at all. If needed, the rest of the body can also move slowly and silently.

After 7½ minutes move the hands in the opposite direction, that is, with the palms down, moving in circular motions inward towards the body. Move the hands for another 7½ minutes. As the hands move outward, feel energy moving away from the body and as they circle inward, imagine taking energy in.

Third Stage: Sit absolutely still and quiet.

Nadabrahma II

Bhagwan has created a beautiful variation of *Nadabrahma* for couples. Partners sit facing one another, holding one another's crossed hands. A bedsheet must cover both bodies and it is best with no other clothing. The room should be fairly dark with four small candles giving the only light. A particular incense should be burning that is used only for this meditation and it should be used on each occasion. Facing one another, hands both crossed and clasped, the couple closes the eyes and continues humming for at least 30 minutes. The humming should be done together. After a minute or two the breathing and humming will merge in unison and the energies will be felt to meet and unite.

Prayer Meditation

Praying should just be an energy phenomenon—not a devotion-to-God phenomenon but an *energy* phenomenon.

In stage one you simply become silent, you simply open yourself. You raise both hands, palms uppermost, head up toward the sky, just feeling existence flowing in you. As the energy, or prana, flows down your arms, you will feel a gentle tremor. Be like a leaf in a breeze, trembling. Allow it; help it. Then let your body vibrate with energy and just let whatever happens happen. After two or three minutes, or whenever you feel completely filled, lean down and kiss the earth (stage two). You simply become a vehicle allowing the divine energy to unite with that of the earth. You feel again a flowing with the earth. Earth and Heaven: above and below: yin and yang: male and female. You float . . . you mix . . . you drop yourself completely . . . you become one and merge.

These two stages should be repeated six more times, so that each of the chakras can become unblocked. You can do them more than six times, but if you do less than six you will feel restless and unable to sleep.

It is best to do this prayer at night, in a darkened room, going to sleep immediately afterward. Or it can be done in the morning, but must be followed by 15 minutes rest. This rest is necessary; otherwise you will feel as if you are drunk, in a stupor.

This merging with energy is prayer. It changes you. And when you change the whole existence changes.

Whirling Meditation

This centering technique was originally a Sufi Dervish meditation. It is recommended that no food or drink be taken for three hours before the meditation. Loose clothing and bare feet are best.

The whirling is done on the spot in an counterclockwise direction which, if it proves too powerful, can be changed to clockwise. The right arm is held high, palm upwards, and the left arm is low with the palm facing down. The energy is collected from the heavens by the right hand and returned to the earth by the left. Starting slowly, build up the speed of the whirl until it takes you over. The periphery moves but the witness in the center remains still. Eventually the body will drop on its own. Lie with the bare navel pressed to the earth as if lying on a mother's breasts. Remain still, sinking into the earth, for a minimum of 15 minutes. There is no fixed time for the whirling . . . it can go on for hours.*

---

*All meditations are accompanied by taped music.

Appendix B:
Chronology

1908	Bhagwan's father born in Timarni.
1915	Bhagwan's mother born in Kuchwada.
1931 December 11	Bhagwan's birth.
1934	Bhagwan's paternal grandfather leaves Timarni and settles down with the family in Gadarwara.
1938	Bhagwan's maternal grandfather dies. Bhagwan comes to live with his parents in Gadarwara.
1947	Shashi, Bhagwan's childhood girlfriend, dies.
1950	Bhagwan graduates from high school.
1951	Bhagwan comes to Jabalpur and enrolls in college.
1952	At Saugar, Bhagwan's body falls from the tree while he is in deep meditation.
1953 March 21	Bhagwan's enlightenment under the maulshree tree in Bhanvartal garden at Jabalpur.
1955	Bhagwan graduates from D. N. Jain College with a B.A. in philosophy, and joins Saugar University for M.A.
1957	Bhagwan earns M.A. in philosophy with distinction. Appointed lecturer at Raipur Sanskrit College, Raipur.

1958	Bhagwan joins the faculty of Mahakoshal Arts College of the University of Jabalpur.
1964	Bhagwan holds the first ten-day meditation camp in Rajasthan.
1966	Bhagwan resigns from Mahakoshal Arts College.

1970

April 10–13	Bhagwan introduces Dynamic Meditation for the first time on a visit to Bombay.
June 30	Bhagwan leaves Jabalpur.
July 1	Bhagwan arrives in Bombay.
September 25–October 5	Bhagwan introduces neo-sannyas and initiates six people at Manali. The official beginning of the Neo-Sannyas International Movement.

| 1971 | Bhagwan's mother takes initiation from him. |
| May | "Acharya" title dropped and the name Bhagwan (Bhagwan Shree Rajneesh) adopted. |

1974

March 21	Bhagwan leaves Bombay and arrives in Poona. Shree Rajneesh Ashram founded.
April	Beginning of Bhagwan's discourses. The first series in Hindi on Chapter 16 of the *Bhagavad Gita*.
May	Beginning of Bhagwan's English discourses. The first series, *My Way: The Way of the White Clouds*. Bhagwan stops directing meditations in person.

1975	Emergency declared in India.
August	Beginning of therapy groups at the ashram.
October 19	Bhagwan's father takes initiation from him.
1977	Janata government comes into power.
1978	Bhagwan's parents and family come to live at the ashram.

1979

| February | Beginning of "energy darshans." |

June 11–20	Bhagwan, due to ill health, stops discourses and darshans. Silent music meditation with Bhagwan.
September 8	Bhagwan's father attains the state of enlightenment and leaves his body (dies).
December 11	Inauguration of the new commune Rajneeshdham at Jadhavwadi, Saswad, near Poona.

1980

January	Mrs. Indira Gandhi and her Congress Party come back into power.
May 22	An assassination attempt on Bhagwan's life.

1981

January 9–10	Swami Anand Vimalkirti (formerly Prince Welf of Hanover) attains the state of enlightenment and leaves his body (dies).
March 23	Bhagwan's last darshan with disciples.
March 24	Bhagwan's last morning discourse. A few cases of chicken pox spotted at the ashram. Morning discourses of Bhagwan and evening darshans cancelled.
March 25	Beginning of silent music meditation without Bhagwan's physical presence.
April 10	Announcement of Bhagwan's entering into the ultimate, silent stage of his work; of his stopping discourses and not being present physically at evening darshans (Ma Yoga Laxmi, Swami Ananda Teertha, and Swami Satya Vedant to function as Bhagwan's medium at darshan).
May 1	Beginning of satsang, the silent communion between the Master and the disciples.
May 27	Fire at Rajneeshdham in Jadhavwadi.
May 28	Explosions and fire at the Rajneesh Foundation book warehouse near Poona. Explosive device detonated at the Foundation's medical center.

June 1   Bhagwan's last silent satsang with disciples;
              leaves Poona in the afternoon to receive
              medical treatment in the United States.

Notes

Introduction

1. Bhagwan Shree Rajneesh, *Dimensions Beyond the Known,* trans. Sadhu Anand Chit, ed. Ma Ananda Prem (Los Angeles: Wisdom Garden Books, 1979), p. 30.
2. Ibid., pp. 30–31.
3. Ibid., p. 31.

Chapter 1: Who Is Bhagwan Shree Rajneesh?

1. *Rajneesh Foundation Press Office Information Files* (Poona, 1975–1981). (Unless othewise noted, the quoted words of Bhagwan in this chapter are taken from the Rajneesh Foundation Press office files).
2. A *darshan* is a gathering in which a small group of *sannyasins* sit near Bhagwan and during which newcomers may take *sannyas* (initiation into disciplehood) from him.
3. The *mala* or necklace is made of 108 wooden beads which represent 108 known techniques of meditation.
4. An *ashram* or monastery is a place where disciples live with a master, work, and meditate.

Chapter 2: Birth and Family

1. Dadda's father's family were followers of a small sect called *Taran Panth.* The sect was founded in the sixteenth century by a saint named Taran Swami, who was a contemporary of the Indian saints Kabir and Nanak. The Jain religion, founded by Mahavir, contemporary of Buddha, was later split into two sects: Digambara and Shwetambara. Taran Swami belonged to the former. The Digambara sect was split further into several small sects, one of which was known as Parwar. Taran Swami's family came from the Parwar sect, which is primarily located in the state of Madhya Pradesh. Taran Swami opposed the idol worship widely prevalent among Digambara Jains and preached the worship of the formless. He criticized the emphasis the Digambara Jains placed on materialism and exhorted them to turn toward the spirituality taught by Mahavir. Taran

Swami was put to a lot of trouble and harassment by the society for his views. However, a few Jains and other non-Jains became his followers. Dadda's forefathers were among those who had accepted Taran Swami as their guru. His teachings are contained in fourteen books. It is said that Bhagwan read his works as a child and may have been inspired by his teachings.

2. The word "Dada" in Hindi means "grandfather," while "Dadda" is used for "elder brother."

3. *The Book of the Secrets,* vol. 4 (Poona: Rajneesh Foundation, 1976), p. 396.

4. Second among the three brothers; the last one is Shikharchand, who later became a disciple of Bhagwan, his own nephew.

5. The city of Jabalpur is halfway between Bombay and Calcutta, about five hundred miles northeast of Bombay. The Narmada River passes close by the city.

6. *Brahma Muhurta* is the holy time, early before sunrise.

7. *Man hi Pooja, Man hi Dhoop,* Hindi discourse, October 2, 1979, translated by the author (Poona: Rajneesh Foundation).

8. Ibid.

9. "O Samadhi Alleluia!" *Sannyas,* no. 6, ed. Ma Yoga Sudha (Poona: Rajneesh Foundation, 1979), p. 45.

10. As the tradition went, the members of the family considered it inauspicious for the bride to see the bridegroom's face before the nuptial rites were over. Marriage ceremonies in those days generally lasted between three and seven days.

11. The bridegroom was brought on horseback to the bride's home in a procession with local bands providing the music.

12. An indication of Bhagwan's being a great soul came once before his birth. When Bhagwan's mother was in her sixth month, her cousin came to bring her to Kuchwada for delivery. The monsoon was at its peak and the river Narmada, which runs between Timarni and Kuchwada, was flooding its banks. The boatman refused to take them across the rising river. Helpless, Bhagwan's mother and her cousin spent three days near the river waiting for the waters to recede. On the third day a tall and very impressive looking monk passed by and found them waiting. Seeing the boatman still reluctant, the monk told him that the lady was due to give birth to a great soul. The monk assured the boatman that no harm whatsoever would occur and hence he should take both of them across without any fear. The boatman trusted the monk's words and took them across the dangerously high river without any difficulty.

13. *Dimensions Beyond the Known,* p. 152.

14. Interviewed at Shree Rajneesh Ashram, Poona.

15. *Dimensions Beyond the Known,* p. 74.

16. Ibid., p. 75.

17. *Yoga: The Alpha and the Omega: Discourses on the Yoga Sutras of Patanjali,* vol. 4 (Poona: Rajneesh Foundation, 1977), p. 203.
18. Ibid.
19. Ibid., p. 204.
20. *Dimensions Beyond the Known,* p. 72.
21. Ibid., p. 68.
22. Ibid., pp. 68–69.
23. Ibid., p. 69.
24. Ibid., pp. 78–79.

Chapter 3: Youth: The Years of Adventure

1. Interview.
2. *The Book of the Secrets: Discourses on "Vigyana Bhairava Tantra,"* vol. 2 (New York: Harper & Row, 1979), p. 196.
3. *Dimensions Beyond the Known,* pp. 152–153.
4. *The Book of the Secrets,* vol. 2, pp. 196–197.
5. *Dimensions Beyond the Known,* pp. 149–150.
6. Ibid., pp. 154–155.
7. Ibid., p. 153.
8. Ibid., p. 154.
9. Ibid., pp. 154, 155.
10. Ibid., p. 155.
11. "Be Still and Know," discourse no. 18, September 18, 1979 (Poona: Rajneesh Foundation).
12. *Dimensions Beyond the Known,* pp. 157–158.
13. Ibid., pp. 158–159.
14. *Only One Sky: On the Tantric Way of Tilopa's Song of Mahamudra* (New York: Dutton, 1976), p. 4.
15. Swami Anand Yatri, *The Sound of Running Water: A Photo-biography of Bhagwan Shree Rajneesh and His Work 1974–1978* (Poona: Rajneesh Foundation, 1980), p. 14.
16. Interview.
17. *And the Flowers Showered: Talks on Zen Stories* (Poona: Rajneesh Foundation, 1975), p. 112.
18. *The Book of the Secrets,* vol. 2, p. 197.
19. Ibid.
20. Ibid., p. 198.
21. Ibid.
22. Ibid.
23. Ibid.
24. *The Grass Grows by Itself: Bhagwan Shree Rajneesh Talks on Zen* (Poona: Rajneesh Foundation, 1976), pp. 117–118.
25. Interview.
26. Subhash Chandra Bose, also known popularly as Netaji, was born in 1897. He was opposed to Mahatma Gandhi's idea of "nonvio-

lence." He led the Indian National Army in 1943 against the British India Government in an attempt to gain independence for India. He died in 1945 in a plane crash.

27. RSS was organized in the 1930s as a Hindu nationalistic movement to revive the cultural heritage of the Hindus.
28. Interview.
29. "Tao: The Golden Gate," discourse no. 18, typed (Poona: Rajneesh Foundation, 1980), pp. GG 18.6–18.7.
30. Shyam Soni, *Jyotishikha,* no. 11 (Jabalpur: Yuvak Kranti Dal, 1968), p. 29.
31. *The Discipline of Transcendence,* vol. 3 (Poona: Rajneesh Foundation, 1978), pp. 206–207.
32. "Be Still and Know," discourse no. 6, September 6, 1979.
33. Ibid.
34. From a Hindi discourse of July 18, 1979, translated by the author (Poona: Rajneesh Foundation).
35. *Dimensions Beyond the Known,* p. 163.
36. A hill resort in the state of Madhya Pradesh.
37. *Jyotishikha,* no. 11 (1968), p. 21.
38. From a Hindi discourse of October 2, 1979, translated by the author.
39. Ma Yoga Vivek, who presently looks after Bhagwan, is said to be Shashi reincarnated in her body. More on her story in Chapter 5.
40. *Dimensions Beyond the Known,* pp. 154–157.
41. Ibid., pp. 155–156.
42. Ibid., p. 156.
43. Ibid.
44. Ibid., p. 157.

Chapter 4: Enlightenment

1. *Dimensions Beyond the Known,* p. 160.
2. *Tao: The Pathless Path,* vol. 2 (Poona: Rajneesh Foundation, 1979), pp. 295–296.
3. Ibid., pp. 296–297.
4. The Aurvedic system is the Indian system of medicine; a trained and qualified practitioner is known as *vaidya.*
5. *Tao: The Pathless Path,* vol. 2, pp. 322–323.
6. Ibid., p. 297.
7. Samadhi: State of trance; state of meditation in which the connection between the body and mind is suspended; at a deeper level a state of being in which the self exists in pure consciousness and bliss.
8. *The Sound of Running Water,* pp. 26–27.
9. *Tao: The Pathless Path,* vol. 2, p. 298.
10. *Dimensions Beyond the Known,* p. 161.
11. *Jyotishikha,* no. 27, ed. Ma Yoga Kranti and Swami Krishna Kabir

(Bombay: Jeevan Jagruti Kendra, 1972), pp. 56–58 (translated from Hindi by the author).

12. *Rajneesh Foundation Press Office Information Files* (Poona: 1975–1981).
13. Author of the *Yoga Sutras,* a treatise on yoga and meditation, c. 150 B.C.
14. Kranti, in her description, has recalled that Bhagwan came back at 3:00 A.M.
15. *The Discipline of Transcendence: Discourses on the Forty-Two Sutras of Buddha,* vol. 2 (Poona: Rajneesh Foundation, 1978), p. 301–310.
16. *The Sound of Running Water,* p. 29.
17. *Take It Easy,* vol. 1 (Poona; Rajneesh Foundation, 1979), pp. 169–170.
18. Ibid., p. 176.
19. *The Discipline of Transcendence,* vol. 2, pp. 313–314.
20. Ibid., p. 314.
21. *The Discipline of Transcendence,* vol. 4 (Poona: Rajneesh Foundation, 1978), p. 107.
22. Ibid.
23. Chapter 14.5–14.27. Bhagwan's discourses on the *Bhagavad Gita* in Hindi contain an explanation of *gunas* in much detail.
24. *Dimensions Beyond the Known,* p. 174.
25. Ibid.
26. Ibid., p. 176.
27. Ibid., p. 178.
28. Ibid.
29. Ibid., p. 176.
30. Ibid., p. 177.
31. Ibid., p. 178.
32. Ibid., pp. 178–179.
33. *Bhagavad Gita,* 2:69.
34. *Dimensions Beyond the Known,* p. 180.
35. Ibid., pp. 181–182.
36. Ibid., p. 183.
37. Ibid.
38. *Vedanta: Seven Steps to Samadhi* (Poona: Rajneesh Foundation, 1976), pp. 192–193.

Chapter 5: Neo-Sannyas: The Lotus in a Swamp

1. *Come Follow Me: Talks on Sayings of Jesus,* vol. 3 (Poona: Rajneesh Foundation, 1977), pp. 214–215.
2. Bhagwan is referring here in good humor to the austerity followed by the ancient Indian sages known as *rishis.*

3. "Zen: Zest, Zip, Zap, and Zing," discourse no. 2, December 20 (Poona: Rajneesh Foundation, 1980).

4. *Dimensions Beyond the Known,* p. 184.

5. Ibid., pp. 184–185.

6. Ibid., p. 185.

7. Ibid., pp. 185–186.

8. *The Orange Book: The Meditation Techniques of Bhagwan Shree Rajneesh,* ed. Swami Veetmoha (Poona: Rajneesh Foundation, 1980), pp. 2–3.

9. Ibid., pp. 26–27.

10. "Tao: The Golden Gate," discourse no. 16, typed (Poona: Rajneesh Foundation, 1980), pp. 16–17.

11. *Dimensions Beyond the Known,* p. 95.

12. Ibid., p. 103.

13. Ibid., p. 92.

14. Gandhi used this term to mean serving the poor as if the poor were God. *Daridra* = poor; *narayan* = God.

15. "The Secret of Secrets," discourse no. 20, typed (Poona: Rajneesh Foundation, 1978), pp. 11–12.

16. *From Sex to Superconsciousness* (Poona: Rajneesh Foundation, 1973), pp. 32–35.

17. *Jyotishikha,* no. 13 (1969), p. 87 (translated from Hindi by the author).

18. *Dimensions Beyond the Known,* p. 185.

19. *Dekh Kabira Roya,* translated from Hindi by the author (Poona: Rajneesh Foundation, 1979), pp. 244–248.

20. *The Ultimate Alchemy: Discourses on the Atma Pooja Upanishad,* vol. 1 (Poona: Rajneesh Foundation, 1974), p. 158.

21. Bhagwan explains the meaning and technique of Dynamic Meditation as follows:

> Dynamic Meditation is a contradiction. "Dynamic" means effort—much effort, absolute effort. And "Meditation" means silence, no effort, no activity. You can call it a dialectical meditation.
>
> Be so active that the whole energy becomes a movement; no energy is left static in you. . . . Become dynamic. . . . You are more like energy. . . . Bring total energy to work. . . .
>
> When everything is moving and you have become a cyclone, then become alert. Remember, be mindful—and in this cyclone suddenly you will find a center which is absolutely silent. This is the center of the cyclone. This is you—you in your divinity, you as a god.
>
> Effort and effortlessness, movement and no movement, activity and no activity, matter and the soul—these are the banks. And between these two flows the invisible. These two are visibles. Between these two flows the invisible—that is what you are. . . .
>
> My system of Dynamic Meditation begins with breathing, and I suggest ten minutes of chaotic breathing in the first stage of the technique. By chaot-

ic breathing I mean deep, fast, vigorous breathing, without any rhythm. Just taking the breath in and throwing it out . . . as deeply, as intensely as possible. . . .

This chaotic breathing is to create a chaos within your repressed system. Whatever you are, you are with a certain type of breathing. A child breathes in a particular way. If you are sexually afraid, you breathe in a particular way. You cannot breathe deeply because every deep breath hits the sex center. If you are fearful, you cannot take deep breaths. Fear creates shallow breathing.

This chaotic breathing is to destroy all your past patterns. . . . Unless a chaos is created you cannot release your repressed emotions. And those emotions have now moved into the body.

You are not body *and* mind, you are body-mind; you are both together. So whatever is done with your body reaches the mind, and whatever is done with the mind reaches the body. Body and mind are two parts of the same entity.

Deep, fast breathing gives you more oxygen. The more oxygen in the body, the more alive you become, the more animal-like—alive, vibrating, vital. With more oxygen in your blood, more energy is in your cells, your body cells will become more alive. This oxygenation helps to create body electricity—or you can call it "bioenergy." When there is electricity in the body you can move deep within, beyond yourself. The electricity will work within you. . . .

The second step in my technique of Dynamic Meditation is a catharsis. I tell you to be *consciously* insane. Whatever comes to your mind—*whatever* —allow it to express itself; cooperate with it. No resistance: just a flow of emotions. If you want to scream, then scream. Cooperate with it. A deep scream, a total scream, in which your whole being becomes involved is very therapeutic, deeply therapeutic. Many things, many diseases, will be released just by the scream. If the scream is total, your whole being will be in it. . . .

This unburdening is basic, and without it there can be no meditation for man as he is. Again, I am not talking about the exceptions—they are irrelevant.

With this second step, when things are thrown out, you become vacant. And this is what is meant by emptiness: to be empty of all repressions. In this emptiness something can be done. Transformation can happen; meditation can happen.

Then, in the third step, I use the sound *hoo*. Many sounds have been used in the past. Each sound has something specific to do. For example, Hindus have been using the sound *aum*. This may be familiar to you. But I won't suggest *aum*. *Aum* strikes at the heart center, but man is no longer centered in the heart. *Aum* is striking at a door where no one is home.

Sufis have used *hoo*, and if you say *hoo* loudly, it goes deep to the sex center. So this sound is used just as a hammering within. When you have become empty and vacant, this sound can move within you.

The movement of the sound is possible only when you are empty. If you are filled with repressions, nothing will happen. And sometimes it is even dangerous to use any mantra or sound when you are filled with repressions. Each layer of repression will change the path of the sound and the ultimate result may be something of which you never dreamed, something which you never expected, never wished for. You need a vacant mind; only then can a mantra be used.

So I never suggest a mantra to anyone as he is. First there must be a catharsis. This mantra *hoo* should never be done without doing the first two steps. It should *never* be done without them. Only in the third step is this *hoo* to be used—used as loudly as possible, bringing your total energy to it. You are to hammer your energy with the sound.

This *hoo* goes deep down and hits the sex center, and the sex center can be hit in two ways. The first way is naturally. Whenever you are attracted to a member of the opposite sex, the sex center is hit from without. And that hit is also a subtle vibration. . . .

Hoo hits the same center of energy but from within. And when the sex center is hit from within, the energy starts to flow within. This inner flow of energy changes you completely. You become transformed: you give birth to yourself.

You are transformed only when your energy moves in a totally opposite direction. Right now it is flowing out, but then it begins to flow within. Now it is flowing down, but then it flows upward. This upward flow of energy is what is known as *kundalini*. You will feel it actually flowing in your spine . . . and the higher it moves, the higher you will move with it. When this energy reaches the *brahmarandhra* (the last center in you, the seventh center located at the top of the head) you are the highest man possible—what Gurdjieff calls "man number seven."

You are "man number one" when your energy is just at the sex center. When some energy comes to your heart center, you are "man number two": the man of emotion. When some energy moves to the intellect, you are "man number three": a man of the intellect. These are ordinary men— all neurotic in their own way. One man is emotionally neurotic, another bodily neurotic, another is intellectually neurotic. But these three men are just ordinary men.

"Man number four" is one who is trying to move his energy within: the man who is meditating, the man who is making efforts to dissolve his neurosis, divisions and schizophrenia. This is "man number four." And as this energy moves upward and upward, a higher man is created. That higher man will be less neurotic, less schizophrenic, more sane. . . .

These two pulls create schizophrenia: one moment you are pulled to the higher and you are like a saint, and the next moment you are pulled down and you are behaving like an animal. The mind becomes confused. You cannot be an animal wholeheartedly, you cannot be at ease with the animal within you, because the higher possibility, the seed, is there and it goes on challenging you. But you cannot remove the animal. It is there; it is your heritage. So you divide yourself in two. You place the animal part of you in the unconscious, and consciously you identify yourself with your higher possibility, which you are not. This higher possibility is the ideal, the end. Consciously you identify with the end, but unconsciously you remain with the beginning. These two points create conflict. So unless you go beyond man, you cannot go beyond madness. Man *is* madness.

In the third step, I use *hoo* as a vehicle to bring your energy upward. These first three steps are cathartic. They are not meditation but just the preparation for it. They are a "getting ready" to take the jump, not the jump itself.

The fourth step is the jump. In the fourth step I tell you to stop. When I say "Stop!" stop completely. Don't do anything at all because anything you do can become a diversion and you will miss the point. Anything—just a cough or a sneeze—and you may miss the whole thing because the mind has become diverted. Then the upward flow will stop immediately because your attention has moved. . . .

When the energy moves upward you become more and more silent. Silence is the by-product of energy moving upward and tension is the by-product of energy moving downward. Now your whole body will become so silent—as if it has disappeared. You will not be able to feel it. You have become bodiless. And when you are silent, the whole existence is silent because the existence is nothing but a mirror. It reflects you. In thousands and thousands of mirrors it reflects you. . . .

In your silence I will tell you to just be a witness, a constant alertness—not doing anything but just remaining a witness, just remaining with yourself; not doing *anything*—no movement, no desire, no becoming—but just remaining then and there, silently witnessing what is happening.

These first three steps will make you ready to remain with the moment. They will make you aware. That is meditation. In that meditation something happens that is beyond words. And once it happens you will never be the same again; it is impossible. It is a growth. It is not simply an experience, it is a growth.

That is the difference between false techniques and real techniques. With false techniques you may experience something, but then you will fall back again. It was just a glimpse, it was not a growth. This can happen with LSD. You will have a glimpse. This can happen with other techniques. . . .

There are false techniques that are easier to do. They never lead you anywhere. If you are just after experiences you will fall prey to any false technique. A real technique is not concerned with experiences as such, a real technique is concerned with growth. Experiences happen; that is irrelevant. My concern is with growth, not with experiences. . . .

I am not going to force sanity upon you. Rather, I am going to bring out your insanity. When it is pulled out completely, thrown into the wind, sanity will happen to you. You will grow. You will be transformed. That is the meaning of meditation.

After ten minutes of silence, the Dynamic Meditation concludes with ten minutes of celebration—singing, dancing, and expressing whatever bliss or ecstasy is there.

Quoted from: *Rajneesh Foundation Press Office Information Files* (Poona, 1975–1981).

22. *The Orange Book*, p. 28.
23. *Sufis: The People of the Path: Talks on Sufism,* vol. 1 (Poona: Rajneesh Foundation, 1979), pp. 288–289.
24. "The Book of Wisdom," discourse no. 6, February 16 (Poona: Rajneesh Foundation, 1979).
25. *I Say Unto You,* vol. 1 (Poona: Rajneesh Foundation, 1980), pp. 20–21

26. *Yukrand,* nos. 5 and 6 (Bombay: Jeevan Jagruti Kendra, 1970), translated from Hindi by the author.

27. Trans. Dolly Diddee, ed. Ma Ananda Prem (Delhi: Motilal Banarsidas, 1977).

28. The Sanskrit word *sannyas* means "renunciation." In the Hindu tradition it means giving up the worldly or material life and entering into a life of austerity, forbearance, and spiritual work.

29. Quotations taken from the following sources: "Tao: The Golden Gate," discourse no. 10, June 20, typed manuscript (Poona: Rajneesh Foundation, 1980), pp. 12–13; *The Wisdom of the Sands: Discourses on Sufism,* vol. 2 (Poonà: Rajneesh Foundation, 1980), p. 200; *Hallelujah!: A Darshan Diary* (Poona: Rajneesh Foundation, 1981) pp. 51–54, 71–73.

30. "I Am That," discourse no. 6, October 16, typed transcript (Poona: Rajneesh Foundation, 1980), p. 26.

31. Ibid., p. 27.

32. *I Am the Gate: The Meaning of Initiation and Discipleship* (New York: Harper & Row, Perennial Library, 1978), p. 41.

33. "The Book of the Books," vol. 6, discourse no. 4, April 14, typed transcript (Poona: Rajneesh Foundation, 1980), pp. 10–11.

34. *I Am the Gate,* pp. 45–46.

35. Ibid., p. 38.

36. *Sangha:* a group of seekers living together a communal life; a congregation of monks.

37. "The Book of Wisdom," vol. 2, discourse no. 17, February 27 (Poona: Rajneesh Foundation, 1979).

38. *The Sound of Running Water,* p. 78.

39. Translated from Hindi by the author. All four letters were published in *Jyotishikha,* no. 20 (March, 1971), pp. 55–57.

40. To: Shri Mathuraprasad Mishra, Patna.

41. To: Shri Hiralal Ji Kothari, Udaypur.

42. To: Shri Omprakash Agrawal, Jullunder.

43. To: Shri Rajendra, Ludhiana.

44. *Sannyas,* no. 6 (Poona, 1979), p. 44.

45. *The Sound of Running Water,* p. 80.

46. The "hoo" sound used in the third stage of the Dynamic Meditation.

47. Bhagwan was born in Kuchwada.

48. Quoted from: "Love's Returning," an interview with Ma Yoga Vivek, December 17, 1978, *Sannyas,* no. 1, ed. Ma Yoga Sudha (Poona: Rajneesh Foundation, 1979), pp. 34–39.

49. *The Sound of Running Water,* pp. 81–83.

50. "Shree" is a term generally used for respect, much as "Sir" or "Mr." are used in English; but it is also used as a title before the names of deities and revered persons, such as one's guru or master.

51. *The Discipline of Transcendence,* vol. 2, pp. 107–108.
52. Ibid., pp. 99–105.
53. *Sufis: The People of the Path, Talks on Sufism,* vol. 2 (Poona: Rajneesh Foundation, 1980), p. 321.
54. "The Book of the Books," vol. 1, discourse no. 8 (Poona: Rajneesh Foundation, 1979).
55. Another commune named Samarpan was set up in the outskirts of the city called Baroda, 180 miles northeast of Bombay in the state of Gujarat. Some of the sannyasins were sent to this commune. The farm and lodging/boarding were made available by Swami Swarupanand Bharti and Ma Swarupanand Bharti.

   Note: I am indebted to Ma Yoga Laxmi, Swami Yoga Chinmaya, and Ma Yoga Taru for their sharing with me the details of Bhagwan's stay in Bombay for this chapter.

Chapter 6: Shree Rajneesh Ashram Poona: A Place of Confluence

1. *Dimensions Beyond the Known,* p. 186.
2. *The Sound of Running Water,* p. 64.
3. The discourses on the *Bhagavad Gita* were the first after Bhagwan arrived in Poona. His first series of English discourses began in May, 1974, and when published was entitled *My Way: The Way of the White Clouds.* Bhagwan's discourses continued over the next seven years.

   The discourses were held either in Chuang Tzu Auditorium (part of his residence) or in Buddha Hall. Bhagwan was driven to Buddha Hall, a distance of about one hundred yards from his residence called Lao Tzu House. These discourses were totally spontaneous and open to the public.

   It has been estimated that from 1974 to 1981 Bhagwan spoke over 33 million words in his daily discourses and evening darshans, averaging 13,000 words per day, seven days a week. During the same period he answered over 10,000 questions.

   In Hindi, Bhagwan has devoted fourteen volumes to the *Bhagavad Gita* (he has spoken on all eighteen chapters of the *Gita*), ten volumes to Mahavir, and another forty volumes to other Indian mystics. In English he has devoted eighteen volumes to Gautam Buddha, seven to Jesus, eleven to Sufism, twelve to Taoism, and twenty-one volumes to Zen masters and their stories.

   More than 2,500 discourses and darshans have been, or are being, transcribed into a total of 336 books, published by Rajneesh Foundation. Of these, 128 contain his English discourses, 144 his Hindi discourses, and 64 are darshan records.

4. Swami Prem Pramod, "Journey Into Silence," (Poona: Rajneesh Foundation Press Office, 1981), p. 9.
5. From 1975 on therapy groups were also conducted during and after the meditation camp.
6. *Rajneesh Foundation Press Office Information Files* (Poona, 1975–1981).
7. Ibid.
8. Ibid. Quoted from: "The Perfect Master," discourse of July 2, 1978 (Poona: Rajneesh Foundation, 1978).
9. "Bhagwan Shree Rajneesh Tells What Is Really Happening in the Shree Rajneesh Ashram Therapy Groups," P.O. T 7/12/8 (Poona: Rajneesh Foundation Press Office, 1978), pp. 7–8.
10. *Take It Easy: 14 Discourses Based on the Doka of Zen Master Ikkyu,* vol. 1 (Poona: Rajneesh Foundation, 1979), pp. 453–454.
11. *Tao: The Pathless Path,* vol. 2, pp. 481–482.
12. Ibid, p. 495.
13. Swami Anand Subhuti, "An Ordinary Buddha: How the Father of Bhagwan Shree Rajneesh Became Enlightened on the Last Day of His Life," P.O. A 24/10/9 (Poona: Rajneesh Foundation Press Office, 1979), pp. 3–4.
14. *Come Follow Me, Talks on Jesus,* vol. 1 (Poona: Rajneesh Foundation, 1976), p. 269.
15. Press Release: P.O. 45, NR 14, T 20/10, 21-10-78 (Poona: Rajneesh Foundation Press Office, 1978), p. 2.
16. Ibid., p. 3.
17. Ibid., pp. 7–9.
18. Press Release, June 13, 1978 (Poona: Rajneesh Foundation Press Office, 1978).
19. "To the Elected Representatives of the People of India: A Call for Justice from the Rajneesh Ashram in Poona," Press Release no. 15-2-1 (Poona: Rajneesh Foundation Press Office), p. 11.
20. *Rajneesh Foundation Press Office Information Files* (Poona, 1975–1981).
21. "Homo Novus—The New Man," editorial, ed. Ma Yoga Sudha, *Sannyas,* no. 5 (Poona: Rajneesh Foundation, 1979), pp. 2–3.
22. "The Book of the Books," discourse no. 1, June 21 (Poona: Rajneesh Foundation, 1979).
23. Chanting the name of deity, singing devotional songs.
24. "Be Still and Know," discourse no. 9, September 9, 1979.
25. *Ajahoon Chet Ganwar: Paltu Vani,* discourse no. 2, translated from Hindi by the author (Poona: Rajneesh Foundation, 1979).
26. Ibid.
27. *The Book of the Secrets,* vol. 4 (Poona: Rajneesh Foundation, 1976), p. 83.
28. Ibid., p. 84.

29. "This Is Not a Cult, This Is Religion," PO/101 (Poona: Rajneesh Foundation Press Office, 1978).

30. The innovative programs of Rajneesh International Meditation University (RIMU) could not find government support for recognition. In April, 1981, the name of the university was changed to Rajneesh International No-University (RIN-U), and it was announced by the Rajneesh Foundation that:

> Rajneesh International No-University will function in freedom and will not seek recognition from any state, country, government, nation, or educational authority. It is not prepared to compromise its revolutionary approach to education in order to gain official recognition. . . . While not seeking any recognition itself, the No-University will recognize certain schools, colleges, institutes, and universities around the world.

Quoted from: Press Release, NR 190, April 15, 1980.

31. The hurdles created by the bureaucracy did not allow this commune to expand and grow. Consequently, the Rajneesh Foundation made further efforts to acquire land in the area of Kutch (in the western state of Gujarat), as well as in the north, but the efforts were not successful.

32. Quoted from: *My People: A Community to Provoke God* (Poona: Rajneesh Foundation, 1978), pp. 38–41; and "With His Sannyasins at the Shree Rajneesh Ashram in Poona *Bhagwan Shree Ranjeesh* Shares His Vision of the New *Rajneeshdham Neo-Sannyas International Commune:* This Very Body the Buddha; This Very Earth, the Lotus Paradise," P.O. T 8/7/9a (Poona: Rajneesh Foundation Press Office, 1979), pp. 1–5.

33. Press Release, NR 11, October 14, 1978.

34. *Sumiran Mera Hari Karain,* discourse no. 2, May 22, 1980, translated by the author (Poona: Rajneesh Foundation).

35. Press Release, NR 102, May 22, 1980.

Chapter 7: The Silent Sage

1. *Zen: Zest, Zip, Zap and Zing* (Poona: Rajneesh Foundation, 1981), pp. 338–350.

2. Ibid.

3. Ibid.

4. Ibid.

5. September 8 was declared *Mahaparinirvana* Day, to be celebrated annually in memory of Bhagwan's father and Vimalkirti and all those sannyasins who have left their bodies (i.e., who have died) and who will be leaving their bodies in the future.

6. Swami Prem Pramod, "Journey Into Silence," p. 11.

7. *Bahutere Hain Ghat,* translated from Hindi by the author (Poona: Rajneesh Foundation, 1981), p. 46.

8. "News from Poona: Bhagwan Begins the Ultimate Stage: Alleluia!" P.O. 18/4/1 (Poona: Rajneesh Foundation Press Office, 1981), pp. 1–2.

9. Quoted from: "The Silent Sage: Bhagwan Shree Rajneesh Goes into Silence," P.O. A 2/5/1a (Poona: Rajneesh Foundation Press Office, 1981), p.1.

10. A similar bout of chicken pox occurred in the ashram in late 1979 when Bhagwan had stopped his Hindi lectures on November 18 and resumed on December 9.

11. *The Sound of One Hand Clapping:* March 1–23, 1981 (Poona: Rajneesh Foundation, 1981).

12. Even after Laxmi returned from her travels, I was asked to continue to be Bhagwan's medium in darshans along with Teertha.

13. Quoted from: "News from Poona," P.O. 18/4/1, p. 3.

14. Quoted from: "Journey into Silence," A 2/5/1b, p. 10, and "The Silent Sage," P.O. A 2/5/1a, p. 3.

15. *Dimensions Beyond the Known,* p. 186.

16. "The Secret of Secrets," discourse no. 20, August 30, 1978, typed transcript (Poona: Rajneesh Foundation, 1978), pp. 16–17.

17. Press Release, NR 193, May 4, 1981.

18. Press Release, NR 195, May 10, 1981.

19. Press Release, NR 204, May 28, 1981.

20. "The Secret of Secrets," discourse no. 20, typed transcript, pp. 4–6.

21. "The Sound of One Hand Clapping, March 1–23," discourse of March 23, 1981.

22. Quoted from: *Rajneeshdham Neo-Sannyas International Commune,* P.O. T 8/7/9a, pp. 5–6.

Epilogue

1. Robert Wuthnow, "The New Religions in Social Context," in *The New Religious Consciousness,* ed. C. Y. Glock and R. N. Bellah (Berkeley, CA: University of California Press, 1976).

2. Erika Bourguignon, "Culture and the Varieties of Consciousness," in *Religious Movements in Contemporary America,* ed. I. Zaretsky and Mark Leone (Princeton, NJ: Princeton University Press, 1974).

3. *Yoga: The Alpha and the Omega,* vol. 4, p. 139.

4. Ibid., p. 142.

5. Ibid., p. 140.

6. Ibid., pp. 144–145.

7. *Philosophia Perennis,* vol. 1 (Poona; Rajneesh Foundation, 1981), p. 13.

8. "Walking in Zen," discourse no. 2, May 2, 1980 (Poona: Rajneesh Foundation).

9. Ibid.

10. Quoted in Satprem, *Sri Aurobindo or the Adventure of Consciousness,* translated from the French by Tehmi (Pondicherry: Sri Aurobindo Ashram, 1970), p. 284.
11. April 10, 1980.
12. Book Reviews of *The Sound of Running Water* and *The Wisdom of the Sands,* vol. 2 (Bombay), June 7, 1981, p. 70.

Books by
Bhagwan Shree Rajneesh

Published by Harper & Row

I Am the Gate (talks on initiation-discipleship)
Meditation: The Art of Ecstasy (talks on meditation techniques)
The Mustard Seed (talks on the sayings of Jesus)
The Book of the Secrets, Volumes, I, II, & III, & IV (talks on
   tantric techniques)
The Psychology of the Esoteric (talks on esoteric teachings)
Journey Toward the Heart

Published by Dutton

Only One Sky (talks on Tilopa's Song of Mahamudra)

Available Through DeVorss

The Grass Grows by Itself (discourses on Zen stories)
And the Flowers Showered (discourses on Zen stories)

Published by Routledge & Kegan Paul

Roots and Wings (discourses on Zen)
The Supreme Doctrine (discourses on the Kenopanishad)

Published by Wisdom Garden Books

Dimensions Beyond the Known (discourses on discipleship)
Nirvana: The Last Nightmare* (discourses on Zen)

---

*In press

Published by Grove Press

My Way: The Way of the White Cloud (talks based on
  questions)
Hammer on the Rock (darshan diary)
The Great Challenge* (early talks)

Published by Rajneesh Foundation

Discourses on Indian Mystics:

The Beloved, Volumes I & II
Yoga: The Alpha and Omega, Volumes I–X
Vedanta: Seven Steps to Samadhi

Discourses on Buddha:

The Heart Sutra
The Diamond Sutra
The Discipline of Transcendence, Volumes I–IV

Discourses on Tao:

Tao: The Three Treasures, Volumes I–IV
Tao: The Pathless Path, Volumes I & II
The Empty Boat
When the Shoe Fits

Discourses on Hassidic Stories:

The Art of Dying
The True Sage

Discourses on the Songs of Kabir:

Ecstasy: The Forgotten Language
The Path of Love
The Divine Melody
The Revolution
The Fish in the Sea Is Not Thirsty
The Guest

---

*In press

Discourses on Meditation:

The Orange Book

Discourses on the Sufi Way:

Just Like That
Until You Die
Sufis: The People of the Path, Volumes I & II
The Wisdom of the Sands, Volumes I & II
The Perfect Master, Volumes I & II
The Secret
Unio Mystica, Volumes I & II

Discourses on Zen:

Ancient Music in the Pines
This Very Body the Buddha
A Sudden Clash of Thunder
Dang Dang Doko Dang
Neither This Nor That
No Water, No Moon
Nirvana: The Last Nightmare
Returning to the Source
The Search (the Ten Zen Bulls)
Roots and Wings
Zen: The Path of Paradox, Volumes I–III
The First Principle
Zen: The Special Transmission
The Sun Rises in the Evening
The White Lotus

Discourses on Jesus:

Come Follow Me, Volumes I–IV
I Say Unto You, Volumes I & II

Discourses on Tantra:

The Book of Secrets, Volumes IV & V
The Tantra Vision, Volumes I & II
Tantra: The Supreme Understanding

Discourses on Greek Mystics:

The Hidden Harmony
Philosophia Perennis, Volumes I & II

Questions and Answers:

My Way: The Way of the White Clouds
Walk Without Feet, Fly Without Wings and Think Without
   Mind
Be Still and Know
Zen: Zest, Zip, Zap and Zing

Early Talks:

The New Alchemy: To Turn You On
From Sex to Superconsciousness
A Cup of Tea (letters)

Darshan Diaries:

Hammer on the Rock
Above All, Don't Wobble
Nothing to Lose but Your Head
Be Realistic: Plan for a Miracle
Get Out of Your Own Way
Beloved of My Heart
The Cypress in the Courtyard
A Rose Is a Rose Is a Rose
Dance Your Way to God
The Passion for the Impossible
The Great Nothing
God Is Not for Sale
The Shadow of the Whip
Blessed Are the Ignorant
What Is, Is, What Ain't, Ain't
The Further Shore
The Open Secret
The Sun Behind the Sun Behind the Sun
Let Go!
The Buddha Disease
The Zero Experience

For Madmen Only (Price of Admission: Your Mind)
This Is It
Far Beyond the Stars
The No Book
Don't Just Do Something, Sit There
Only Losers Can Win in This Game
The Open Door
Believing the Impossible before Breakfast
The Ninety-nine Names of Nothingness
The Madman's Guide to Enlightenment
Hallelujah!
The Tongue Tip Taste of Tao
Turn on, Tune in and Drop the Lot
The Sound of One Hand Clapping

Books on
Bhagwan Shree Rajneesh

Published by Harper & Row

Dying for Enlightenment by Swami Deva Amitprem (Bernard
 Gunther)
Neo-Tantra by Swami Deva Amitprem (Bernard Gunther)

Published by Routledge and Kegan Paul

Death Comes Dancing: Celebrating Life with Bhagwan Shree
 Rajneesh by Ma Satya Bharti

Published by Grove Press

Drunk on the Divine (Original title: The Ultimate Risk) by Ma
 Satya Bharti

Published by Rajneesh Foundation

The Sound of Running Water
(A photobiography of Bhagwan Shree Rajneesh and his work,
 1974–1976) by Swami Anand Yatri
Lord of the Full Moon: Life with Bhagwan Shree Rajneesh by
 Ma Prem Divya

Rajneesh Meditation Centers

There are hundreds of Rajneesh meditation centers
throughout the world. General information, including the
name and address of the center nearest you, is available
from: Rajneesh Foundation International, P.O. Box 12A,
Antelope, OR 97001, U.S.A.